Thos. Fitch.

Gal. 2[20]

D1349912

STRAIGHT TALKS

STRAIGHT TALKS

Short Addresses Delivered to the Forces

by

THOMAS FITCH,
M.A., B.D., Ph.D., H.C.F.

MARSHALL, MORGAN & SCOTT LTD.
London :: Edinburgh

MARSHALL, MORGAN AND SCOTT, LTD.
LONDON: 33 LUDGATE HILL, E.C.4
EDINBURGH: 31 SHANDWICK PLACE

U.S.A.
VAN KAMPEN PRESS
222 EAST WILLOW STREET
WHEATON
ILLINOIS

CANADA
EVANGELICAL PUBLISHERS
366 BAY STREET
TORONTO

FIRST PUBLISHED 1950

Printed in Great Britain by
THE MARSHALL PRESS LIMITED
7, Milford Lane, Strand, London, W.C.2

CONTENTS

To My Parents

PREFACE

THE short addresses which comprise this volume were all delivered to Service personnel while I was on active service as a chaplain in the Army.

Originally they were preached from notes, and in dictating them for typing I have made every effort to retain the conversational language which was first used in their delivery.

It is impossible for me to pay tribute to all to whom I am indebted for the material which helped in the composition of these addresses, for that material has been gathered from many and varied sources which I cannot now claim to know.

My purpose in sending them forth in this way is twofold. Firstly, that the written word might be used by the Spirit of God to bring young men and women into personal relationship with Jesus Christ. Secondly, that the ministry of these talks might extend to young Christian men and women by helping them in their Christian experience as well as supplying material which they might use in the propagation of the faith.

I am deeply indebted to Mrs. G. Macallan for undertaking the work of noting the addresses in shorthand, typing them, and making valuable suggestions.

ONE

POWER

For I am not ashamed of the Gospel of Christ: for it is the power of God unto salvation to every one that believeth; to the Jew first, and also to the Greek.
—Romans 1:16.

I WANT to speak to you about power. That is something which nearly everyone would like to possess, but we have all seen, in these last years, power possessed and wielded in a wrong way. To-day I am not thinking of it in that sense—I am thinking of power in a good sense, and to narrow the scope of our thought further, thinking of it as spiritual power within the individual.

After hearing me preach one day, a young Glasgow graduate came to me and said, "It's all very well for you to talk as you do, and it is not that I want to disagree with you, but here is my problem: Often when I know what is the right thing to do, want to do it, and start out to do it, I discover that the perversity of my nature comes in, and the very thing that I intended doing, I don't do: and the same has been true about things that I definitely know to be wrong, for oftentimes I have known what was wrong and had no real desire to do it, and yet just as I would turn away from the temptation, the perversity of nature would again appear and I would find myself engaged in that which I had no intention of doing."

I wonder if that young person realized that that statement is simply a modern expression of what Paul said years ago: "The good that I would I do not, but the evil which I would not, that I do" (Rom. 7:19).

From all of which we can conclude that our real problem is not lack of knowledge of what is good or evil, but, once knowing what is good, lack of power to accomplish it. I feel we want to ponder here for a moment, for already I can sense that you have found the same difficulty in your experience.

Let me give you a homely illustration. My charge is in a golfing centre. At first I knew comparatively little about golf, but I realized that if I was not going to suffer from a self-inflicted ostracism I would need to learn something of the game. So a young enthusiast took me in hand and did his very best for me. After a time I knew the rules of the game, and I knew what was expected of me if I would play golf. Yet to-day the position is something like this: I come out to the tee, place my ball, take my stance as I was taught, seek to keep my eye fixed on the ball as I swing my club back with a straight left arm, and then follow through. I am told that if I do that the ball will go where I want it to go. Now, believe it or not, I seldom find that little ball going where I intended that it should go. You see, the point is that I know what is expected of me, I know how to do it, I want to do it, but when I try to do it, I am not able.

In our conflict with evil, most of us realize that while we are prepared to accept good advice, we need something more. Good news that will tell where and how to procure the transmission of power to achieve complete fulfilment of our aims will be welcomed with open arms. Many there are ready to give good advice: no one but God can give the power needed to carry it out. What has been said is summed up in these words of a hymn we often sing:

"Fight the good fight with all thy might."

That is good advice and nothing more, but the second line brings us the good news:

"Christ is thy strength and Christ thy right."

A man who is drowning does not desire someone to read calmly to him all the rules of natation—such advise is fatuous. What he needs is a saviour. To sum up, then, we are thus made aware of the humbling fact of human impotence, face to face with the power of evil.

But now we turn to another side. This text which I have quoted to you speaks of the power of God. Now it seems to me that this man is saying something worth while—something that comes near to us in our need, for he speaks of the power of God unto salvation. I take it that he means that God's power is available for our salvation, and in our human need and impotence that surely is good news.

Think for a moment of the-power-of-God. I like to make this a hyphenated phrase, for power divorced from God can be something that I dread. God divorced from power would make Him impotent, but here is the phrase, "the-power-of-God." There are many ways in which we might visualize this omnipotence—we might think of it in terms of space and try to comprehend in millions of light years what we have been taught to believe separates us from other planets, and as we contemplate it our minds begin to reel and we fail to grasp it, but as we realize in a measure the immensity of space we do well to remember that God is greater than that. Or we may think of God's power in relation to the universe. Sometimes we marvel at the intricacy of human-made machinery, but when we think of all the laws that govern the universe, laws within laws, and the whole running in the most perfect order without ever breaking down—as if it were one huge machine in which were wheels within wheels—never one cog out of place—then it is good to remember that God is greater than all that.

Or another way to look at this divine power, and one that may be more acceptable to us, is when we see God's amazing power in action in the lives of some men, as, for example, when He changed Jacob the twister to Israel the man of power with God and men, Simon the irresponsible to Peter the man of rock-like character, Saul the bigoted Jew to Paul the humble and devoted Christian.

This, then, is the position we have reached. On the one hand, human impotence: on the other, divine omnipotence. Are they of any value to each other? Not as long as they remain thus separated, in the same way as the electric tram is unable to move when disconnected from the power. Human impotence can look up and marvel at divine omnipotence without anything whatever being effected. Divine omnipotence may look down on human impotence and effect nothing.

But have they thus to be kept apart? Surely this man through the text is saying that these two can be brought together. Indeed, the good news that he is out to proclaim is that these two have been brought together in human experience, so that human impotence is swallowed up by divine omnipotence. As Paul on another occasion said: "I can do all things through Christ which strengtheneth me."

How, then, are these two brought together? The verse says that this power is available to everyone that believeth. I have learned in Christian experience that believing really means receiving. In the Christian sense it means receiving Christ. Let me illustrate what I mean.

Following the illustration used earlier in this talk, I ask you to think of a further golfing illustration.

Suppose I seek to pose as the world's most notable golfer. I watch him closely, practise his technique, and then go out and play with his clubs and seek to emulate his style. In a moment it will be seen that I am not the one whom I pretend to be. I stand exposed as a fool. Suppose, then, I manage somehow to get this man of international reputation within me, so that he thinks with my brain, sees through my eyes, makes use of my arms, hands, legs and whole body. Then my performance will be completely different. Because he does it through me. " Fantastic! impossible! " you say. True, but I want to tell you with all solemnity and yet with great joy that this is the secret of all true Christian living. Listen to it as it comes from the words of Scripture: " I live, yet not I but Christ liveth in me." (Gal. 2:20). Or, if you want an authority other than Paul, here is the Master Himself: " I in them, Thou in Me," as He speaks to the Father. Take these words backwards—"Thou in Me, I in them." Don't you see that the glory of the Christian life is this, that the Christian soul is united to God and has Christ's life within? The finite united with the infinite—the impotent with the omnipotent. Mystical and mysterious, you say. Yes, both it may be, but nevertheless real.

Does this interest you? Do you ask this further question, " How then may I know it? " To that I simply reply, " Take this chorus that you possibly sang as a child; repeat it again and act upon its words:

> Into my heart, into my heart,
>   Come into my heart, Lord Jesus.
> Come in to-day, come in to stay,
>   Come into my heart, Lord Jesus."

And if you really allow Him in, this is the promise of the Word of God to you: As many as receive Him, to them gives He the power.

TWO

DIVINE LOVE

" God so loved the world that He gave . . ."—John 3:16.

"THE Church's message," said a lad the other day to me, " ought always to be the love of God "; and there are many who agree, contending that that message would draw men into the Christian way.

It is true that there is no gospel apart from the love of God. The Christian message was born in the heart of One who is Love. But I should like to remind you that not always has the preaching of the love of God been so successful as some suppose.

Take, for example, that Old Testament prophet Hosea, who was taught through his own experience that God loved even wayward Israel. This message he preached in a way that very few could have preached, and yet no one, acquainted with the facts, would say that Hosea's message was tremendously successful.

Nor, to take the most outstanding example of all, that of Jesus Christ Himself. Could one say that His ministry, according to human standards, was outstandingly successful?

And yet I want to speak of it, this great abiding theme, the love of God, to you now. In repeating the well-known verse, John 3:16: "For God so loved the world that He gave His only begotten Son, that whosoever believeth in Him should not perish, but have everlasting life," I usually linger upon that word "So," for it is a word of tremendous expression. It means that there is no limit whatever to the love of God. Somewhere Paul speaks about the height and depth and length and breadth of the love of God, and to me, it is in its height unscaleable, in its depth unfathomable, in its length illimitable, and in its breadth immeasurable. No instrument has yet been devised to measure the intensity of human sentiments, nor can any gauge the intensity of the Divine Love. But this we CAN say; it is deeper in intensity and richer in quality than human love at its highest. Indeed, Divine Love is on an entirely different plane from human love, for human love at best is only a slight echo of the love of God.

> "He gave " . . .
> Love ever gives, forgives, outlives
> And ever stands with open hands,
> And while it lives it gives,
> For this is love's prerogative—
> To give, and give, and give.

The Divine Love withheld not its best. There was no stinting in its giving. It was poured out with a prodigality that only the Divine Heart can achieve.

"He gave His only begotten Son"—that in itself would have meant a great deal, but He gave His Son to die. Let us not forget that He died, not as any other martyr would have died, for never a Christian martyr went to the scaffold or stake without the Divine Presence. He Himself gave His life and went alone, forsaken of God.

Now, Divine Love far surpasses human love. This may be seen in various ways, but think of it in these two aspects.

First, Divine Love makes no mistakes. Human love does. Mother love is the best example of human love we know, yet many a mother, because of the type of love that she has, often spoils a child. But we know that God never makes a mistake, that no child of His that is truly nurtured in His love is ever spoiled.

And secondly, Divine Love never gives way. Human love may, and sometimes does.

> Can a woman's tender care
> Cease towards the child she bear?
> Yes, she may forgetful be,
> Yet will I remember thee.

Human love can break down under the constant pressure of various types of conduct, but God's love never, no matter what our conduct is. Even His judgments are motivated by love and have a remedial intent.

So here we have clearly stated the fact of Divine Love.

But I am concerned to-day not simply with the mere statement of the fact of Divine Love, but also with our individual reaction to it.

I suppose we have all read some love-story where love for one is expressed to another, but the love offered cannot be returned and so has to be rejected.

Yet even the most debased realize that when love is thus offered it is the highest offering that any human can make, and so, though rejected, is nevertheless turned from with an expression of gratitude and sorrow.

And yet do we not treat God in a way less than this? Hear what He says about so many—" Ye have forgotten Me." It seems to me to be a phrase torn from a bleeding heart, for had we never known Him we could never have been expected to turn to Him, but the indictment is that we have forgotten Him.

As we are brought face to face with the Love of God

this day afresh, what is to be our reaction? Some make recognition of His love and say, "He loved me and gave Himself for me," but a mere recognition has no effect whatever upon their life and character. They pass it by, completely unresponsive, and the love of God continues shining, like the sun, both on the rock and the fruitful soil, with different results.

There are others who turn to Him and say, " We love Him because He first loved us." This is the reaction our Lord delights to see.

A story is told of an incident in the life of Sir George Adam Smith while on a visit to Brittany. One day he was travelling in a railway compartment alone, when, at a wayside station a young priest entered. Some conversation ensued, and in the course of that conversation Sir George learned that the young priest was on his homeward way to say farewell to his parents before embarking for mission work in one of the most unhealthy parts of the African continent. He mentioned that in that part of the country to which he purposed going, the average life of a priest was eighteen months, and as he came to his journey's end and prepared to alight at another wayside station, he touched Sir George on the shoulder and said, " You may wonder why I am going out there, as it were, to throw away my life. It is because He loved me and gave Himself for me."

You and I ofttimes sing:

> Were the whole realm of nature mine,
>   That were an offering far too small;
> Love so amazing, so divine,
>   Demands my soul, my life, my all.

But that verse as it stands is only a recognition of the Divine Love, and a realization of what is due to that Love. We need to make it more definite. We need to say not simply *demands* my soul, but *shall have* my soul, my life, my all. This type of reaction to the Divine Love gladdens the heart of the Divine Father.

There is no heart incapable of love, so that none can truthfully say, " It is beyond me."

What, then, shall we say as again we view the Love that is unmistakable, the Love that is undeserved? Might we not all say in the words of this verse of another hymn :

> Lord, it is my chief complaint
> That my love is weak and faint.
> Yet I love Thee and adore,
> Oh, for grace to love Thee more!

THREE

THE EXPERIENCE OF FORGIVENESS

" Blessed is he whose transgression is forgiven, whose sin is covered."—Psalm 32:1.

SUPPOSE, for a moment, that some trouble has arisen between a husband and wife. A barrier has been erected between them and the whole of their former relationship has been impaired. Their love for each other has received a heavy blow. The influence of it extends to the relationships in the home. Dispeace has taken the place of peace. Disharmony has entered where before harmony existed. Unhappiness is felt, contentment has gone, and the general atmosphere of home has completely changed.

In the case we are thinking of, both are sensible people. The husband, coming to himself, realizes that he is mainly responsible for this state of affairs, and seeks, with true humility, forgiveness, which is readily granted to him. Almost immediately, the relationship that was broken is restored. Happiness is once more evident in the individual, and in the home everything is again harmonious and there is a song and buoyancy in life, and the evidence of love is seen on every hand. Such an illustration reveals that forgiveness brings not merely itself, but produces many other wonderful blessings.

Now, something like that takes place, but in a far more extensive way, when we receive the forgiveness of God.

Some of you ask, "Is there any need of forgiveness?" I do not stay to argue the question. I only ask this further question, "Why does God talk about it so much?" Why does He make offer of it, and why the Cross of Jesus Christ? The only answer that seems to me adequately to meet these questions is that whether we believe it or not, God, who is desperately in earnest about this business, knows that we need forgiveness and longs to give it. It is evident, I judge, that there is little consciousness of sin in our day and generation: but oh, how the sincere Christian longs that conviction would come upon mankind and may it please the Spirit to use this word to bring conviction to some. Never let us forget that we are sinners all, without any exception, and that we need forgiveness and that forgiveness can only be received from God in and through Jesus Christ.

Here are a few of the Scriptures that remind us of our need and of the mercy and loving kindness of God.

"Come now and let us reason together, saith the Lord, though your sins be as scarlet they shall be white as snow, though they be red as crimson they shall be as wool." In this verse we are exhorted to believe that no matter how deep-dyed may be our sin its stain can all be clean erased from our record.

"As far as the east is from the west, so far hath He removed our transgressions from us," and there we have the promise of sin being completely taken away, reminding us of the New Testament word, "Behold the Lamb of God which taketh away the sin of the world."

Moreover, God has promised to put our sins behind His back, never to be remembered any more or drowned in the depth of the sea. What an amazing promise is this! Sins forgiven are completely forgotten by God. Others will remember—but He forgets.

Or, turning to the New Testament, "In whom we have redemption through His blood, even the forgiveness of sins."

"If we confess our sins, He is faithful and just to forgive us our sins and to cleanse us from all unrighteousness." Thus the Old and New Testaments combine in the declaration that forgiveness is real.

Don't you think that the Scriptures are endeavouring by every type of metaphor to make the offer of God clear to man? Words tumble over words as if by this process they might call attention to this amazing fact.

I suppose this first verse of the psalm could be translated this way: "Oh, the blessednesses of the man whose transgression is forgiven and whose sin is covered."

You see, the facts of experience seem to point to this, that there is something between God and the individual, and the Scriptures come and say, "Your sins have separated you"; but when sin is forgiven, oh, the blessedness that comes with it, because the true relationship between God and the individual is restored. In other words, we are at peace with God. And God is constantly offering in Christ forgiveness to every human soul, for it is only in and through Christ's death that it has been made possible.

But this forgiveness, to be enjoyed, must be received. I can go on offering forgiveness to one who may not want to receive that forgiveness, and the true relationship can never in that way be restored. And so, too, with God. He continues to offer, but man must accept, and He never bludgeons man into acceptance. Man must come of his own free will.

In the fifth verse of the psalm the psalmist said, " I acknowledged my sin unto Thee and mine iniquity have I not hid."

That is the true spirit in which to come before God and receive His forgiveness.

Yet so few come acknowledging their sin. Despite the way provided whereby forgiveness may be secured they do not simply hesitate to come, but they refuse to come. Conceiving God as some easy-going benevolent old gentleman who will see them all right no matter what happens, they persist in their own way and fail to come in the divinely appointed way.

Do not make any mistake. Forgiveness is offered to you. But it is offered on God's terms. Come confessing your need of it and receive it, and then you will discover the priceless blessedness and rapture of it.

The full content of forgiveness only becomes known as it is gradually experienced. With it we become at one with God. Lost peace is restored, harmony again exists, contentment is experienced in life and love is at its best. Thus the glory of forgiveness is made real.

And so there it is: God's offer has not yet been withdrawn—but have we accepted it?

FOUR

THE FRIENDSHIP OF CHRIST

A FEW years ago at Keswick Convention, I heard Dr. Barnhouse, of America, tell a story which was something like this.

From a nearby college a young professor came to ask for his advice. As they sat together in the study, Dr. Barnhouse told the young professor the following story:

There was a man who had lived a rather dissolute life, but one day Jesus Christ met him and the whole of his life was changed. Some time after his conversion he was introduced to a Christian young woman and they became friends.

During the course of their friendship this man felt that it was only right that he should explain to this young woman the type of life that he had lived in the past, and with some fear and trembling he did so. The young woman, however, felt that he was truly converted and that he was also God's chosen partner for her life, and in due course they were married.

Not long after their marriage, the young wife came to her husband and said, "You were gracious enough to tell me something of your past history. I know something of Christian experience, and I know something of the ways of the Evil One. I feel, therefore, that you will be tempted along the line of your past sin. I want you to realize that if ever you *are* tempted to give way, and I pray God that that may never take place, but if you should be tempted and give way "

—and again she said, " I pray God that that may never take place "—" I want you to realize that even although the tempter may say, ' What's the use of going back home? '—that this IS your home and here there will always be a welcome for you. When I married you I married you, your past, what you are, and all your future."

The young professor, who had listened to this story without raising his head, with a certain passionate note in his voice, exclaimed, " My God, if anything would make a man go straight, THAT should."

I tell you this story because I think that it is a story of real friendship. You say it is a story of real love. Yes, but there is no true friendship that is not based on love. There is no more solid foundation upon which to build the structure of friendship than the foundation of love. And the friendship of Christ is based upon eternal love.

> Which of all our friends to save us
> Could or would have shed his blood?
> But the Saviour died to have us
> Reconciled in Him to God.
> This was boundless love indeed—
> Jesus is a Friend in need.

Let me say three things concerning the friendship of Christ. I gather them from different sources. First:

A perfect friend is one who knows the worst about you and loves
    you just the same;
There's only One who loves like this, and Jesus is His name.

That constitutes one of the great aspects of the friendship that Christ offers to men. He knows all about us and yet continues to love us. He knows us at our best, and we know that that is never very estimable. He knows us at our worst, and we know how low we can sometimes sink, and yet—oh, the wonder of it!—He still continues to love us.

Human friendships are occasionally lost because of unexpected traits of character which sometimes appear in another or in ourselves. And so friendships are broken. He, however, refuses to allow His friendship to be broken down, no matter how we treat Him—no matter what we do to Him. Your remember how He calls those who would follow Him "friends, not servants"—you remember how it is truthfully said of Him, "A friend of publicans and sinners." How glad I am of that title, for it includes me, and yet He who was a Perfect Friend to all with whom He came into contact knew a great deal of the faithlessness of friends. For it is recorded, "Many went back and walked no more with Him." But that friendship which they spurned and which to-day is often spurned, is never withdrawn, for it is ever being offered to wayward humanity and so to each of us.

Secondly, Transforming Friendship. I take this title from a book of Leslie Weatherhead's which I remember to have seen among my father's books many years ago. A book into which I looked, but never fully read. That which remains with me to-day is its name— "Transforming Friendship." And this is true of all the friendship of Christ. It may be true to say that ALL friendship transforms. Sometimes it works for good, at other times for evil. Too often we have seen those who have been walking the way that is right meeting with people who have befriended them who were walking the way that is wrong, and that friendship was the means by which their lives were changed and marred and ruined. But thank God we have also seen those who, walking the road that leads to destruction, were met by people who were walking the road that leads to life and whose subsequent friendship meant that the former were turned and in the end transformed. Yes, human friendship is, in a measure, friendship that transforms, but this friendship of Christ is always transforming and always for good. It is a friendship that transcends every type of human friendship. For there is no man who will make company long with Jesus Christ but will realize the change that comes over him. Make a trial of it in this way: Walk with Him for a month or so, take stock of your life now and at the end of that period, compare both, and I am confident that you will discover such a transformation as can only be explained by recognizing it as the influence of the friendship of the indwelling Christ.

Just take one example. Many fiery-tempered souls like the sons of Boanerges have been mellowed into characters of love and unhurried quietness. I sometimes marvel at many people who would, in normal circumstances, be considered uneducated and illiterate who, because of their constant life in the company of Jesus and of His Word, bear about with them a quiet dignity and a sure knowledge.

Thirdly:

> What a Friend we have in Jesus,
>   All our sins and griefs to bear,
> What a privilege to carry
>   Everything to Him in prayer.

It is the phrase, "Everything to Him in prayer," that I wish to emphasize. No matter what it is, there is nothing, whether small or great that we cannot talk over with Him. There are some things in life that we just cannot tell to another. The husband withholds something from his wife and the wife retains something within herself that is never told to the husband. But the glory of the friendship of Christ is that there is nothing—nothing—that we need withhold from Him. As we unburden ourselves to Him, He knows and understands and helps. Listening one day to a preacher in York, I heard him say that on one occasion during an itinerary that he was making, he was lodged in the house of a lady who was famous for a diary that she had written. One day he was asked by her if he would care to read the diary. It was an opportunity that he had hoped might come his way, and he accepted it with gratitude, so she brought to him the famous diary. As he took it from her, he noticed that there were several pages drawn together by little blue ribbons tied in little bows. "Now," he said, looking at his audience, "what would you do in circumstances like that? So," he continued, " I began to untie the little bows, but the lady, who was watching, put forward her hand and said, ' No, no, not that part; that is my own private part.' "

That, surely, is true of all. There is that part of our personality that is known only to ourselves—not even our nearest or our best ever penetrate into the secrets that it holds, but oh, the wonder of it!—it can all be laid open and bare to the friendship of Christ. This, to me, is one of the great benefits of the Christian Faith. Friendship with Christ—a friendship in which nothing is withheld from Him, a friendship without a secret.

Do we know this friendship? I can offer friendship to others and it can mean nothing to them because they refuse to accept it. To know friendship it must be reciprocated. In other words, friendship, to be complete or full, must have the cycle of friendship completed.

Jesus Christ is offering Himself to each as a Friend. He withholds Himself from none. But to know Him as a Friend we must accept Him and give ourselves in return, withholding nothing.

Alfred Legge's hymn in the final words of each verse sums up this relationship in its proper order:

> Rest of the weary,
>   Joy of the sad,
> Hope of the dreary,
>   Life of the glad;
> Home of the stranger,
>   Strength to the end,
> Refuge from danger,
>   Saviour and Friend.

These last two words give the true order—" Saviour and Friend." It is when Christ becomes OUR Saviour that we, too, know Him as Friend.

FIVE

TEMPTATION

THERE are many people who have asked me about this subject. What I have to say has particular reference to Christian people.

At the beginning let us realize this—that the unconverted man does not experience temptation to the same extent as the man who has come to know Jesus Christ for himself. To make a decision for Christ means that we stand by Christ in His opposition to all the evil that the Devil produces. And so the Evil One does everything in his power to bring about the downfall of every Christian.

Or, to put it in this way, before a man becomes a Christian he is, as it were, floating downstream along with the crowd. It is so easy, all go together, there is little or no opposition. But immediately he begins facing upstream he has then to pit his strength against the current.

It is also true that the deeper our experience of Jesus Christ, the greater become our temptations. That, of course, includes more opportunities for victory. In this respect it becomes evident that our Lord was the most tempted Man of all.

There are temptations in every phase of life. They may change with the passage of years, but there is not an age, as far as I can gather, in which the power of temptation is not felt.

Because of this I would suggest to you that if at any time you hear of, or know of, a man of Christian stand-

ing yielding to temptation, that you do not despise him
or criticize him, but rather remember, because of his
standing, the strength of the opposition or temptation
that he has had to face before he ultimately gave way.

One point that is worth remembering is that there are
two aspects of temptation mentioned in Scripture. The
first is that in which God tests. In this respect God
seeks to test the worth of a man in the same way as the
goldsmith would seek to test his metal, or the rope-
maker would seek to test his rope. But God does not
tempt to sin.

The second is where Satan initiates the tempting,
and where his whole effort is to solicit to sin. It may
not be possible in our experience to distinguish between
these two, but each of them constitutes a challenge to
us and even that in which Satan seeks to work our
overthrow is still under the control of God, "who is
faithful and will not suffer you to be tempted above
that ye are able, but will with the temptation also make
a way of escape that ye may be able to bear it" (1
Cor. 10:13).

Temptation is not sin. Our Lord was tempted in
all points like as we are, yet without sin (Heb. 4:15). In
a measure we are not responsible for temptation. No
matter what we do or where we go it will appear, but
there is no need that we should yield to it. There is
an old saying which runs like this: "We are unable to
keep the birds from flying over our head, but we can
keep them from building nests in our hair." So with
temptations. We cannot keep them from appearing,
but we can refuse to give them room. Temptation only
becomes sin when in mind we have yielded to it. That
does not necessarily mean that an outward act has to

be committed before we have sinned, for our Lord makes it very clear in His teaching that a great deal of sin is committed within the heart. He taught very definitely the inwardness of sin. If we treasure within our lives wrong and unclean thoughts, if we have determined upon a certain course even although the opportunity has not presented itself for pursuing that course, yet in purposing it we have sinned.

The hymn that we have all sung is true when it says: " Yield not to temptation, for yielding is sin."

It may be that some young Christian asks me, " But why DO we yield to temptation and so sin when at times we have a real desire to overcome? " I think the only answer to that is that at the requisite moment we have failed to take the way of escape provided for us. I feel, for example, that Judas, right up to the last moment, had an opportunity of turning away from his traitorous purpose. Some have suggested that when our Lord gave the sop to Judas, He was making one last effort to win his friendship. Or it might be regarded as a loving endeavour to strengthen him against temptation, but the tragedy of Judas' life is that, at the very moment that Jesus endeavoured so to help him, he permitted Satan to enter his heart.

Before we pass on, let us notice that yielding to temptation vastly weakens our defences for any other onslaught. Let me picture it in this way: Our life is surrounded by a defence through which the enemy of our souls is constantly seeking to find a way. When the defence at any point is broken down by our participation in some sin, a new track into our souls has been made, and it is one of the most difficult things in all experience to rebuild the defence that is thus broken down.

Then victory strengthens us for further gains. Here again the hymn agrees with us—

"Each victory will help us some other to win."

Victory strengthens in different ways. It strengthens our general moral tone, and it strengthens us by the joy that it brings when some severe temptation has been overcome. So that when it appears again, we can remember the joy that there is in victory and it helps us to see the temptation in its true light.

What, then, is the secret of victory? I have already said that there is a sense in which we are not responsible for the temptations with which we are assailed, but I want to modify that statement by saying that there is another sense in which we share responsibility for the temptations that come to us.

Where do we allow our footsteps to lead us? If it is into the pathway where, for us, temptation lurks, then surely we can blame no one else but ourselves when we discover ourselves battling against heavy odds. What do we permit our eyes to see? If we store up in the picture gallery of our minds that which will definitely arouse the evil and the passions within us, then whom else dare we blame but ourselves when we are face to face with temptation?

And the same, surely, is true of what we read. Too often we feed the flame that we say we want to extinguish. Here Scripture reminds us of the same thing— "Make no provision for the flesh to fulfil the lusts thereof."

So the first thing I would say is, guard the gates which protect the city of man's soul.

Secondly, I would say, occupy your mind. If it is true that Satan finds something for idle hands to do, it is also true that he will fill up the mind with much that is evil if we do not fill it up with that which is good. It may not be easy, but it is a practice well worth adopting when we become conscious of any evil thought in possession of our mind, to turn away from it with one strong, deliberate act of the will. Do what the apostle suggests should be done in Philippians 4:8: "Whatsoever things are true, whatsoever things are honest, whatsoever things are just, whatsoever things are pure, whatsoever things are lovely, whatsoever things are of good report, if there be any virtue and if there be any praise, think on these things."

Thirdly. A third practical suggestion is that we should, as it were, pray in advance. What I mean is that at the moment when we are not faced with temptation we should definitely pray that, since now we want to overcome all temptation, when temptation does appear and may appear in such a way that we shall not be keen to overcome, God, by His grace, may answer the prayer that has been made in our better moments and so preserve us from sin.

Fourthly, the most important suggestion of all, and that without which the others cannot properly be fulfilled, is to live much in the presence of Jesus Christ. As we keep close to Him we are helped, in a measure, to have the mind of Christ, and so thus to see sin as it actually is, to know the results of sin for what they are, and to have a real hatred for the thing that would not only harm our own lives but hinder the work of God. According to Psalm 91, it is when we dwell—make our abode—in the secret place of the Most High that we are promised, "Thou shalt tread upon the lion and adder: the young lion and the dragon shalt thou trample under feet."

I know of no way whereby to overcome temptation and to live the life of victory that is promised to us in the New Testament than by being wholly His and living much with Him.

SIX

REPENTANCE

JOHN THE BAPTIST, following the line of the Old Testament prophets, suddenly burst forth upon his day and generation with the message, "Repent, for the kingdom of heaven is at hand." When Jesus Himself appeared following immediately upon John, His message, too, was one of repentance. Later in His ministry, when Jesus sent His disciples forth, it is recorded of them that they went and preached everywhere that men should repent.

To read the record of the early Church is to be faced with the fact that the apostles proclaimed the same thought, and when the risen Christ speaks to the Church at Ephesus through His apostle John, the emphasis again is laid upon the word "Repent."

I feel, then, in coming to you with this message, that I am following in a good succession, and I would ask you to note the urgency that is attached to this subject. "Except ye repent, ye shall all likewise perish" (Luke 13:3). It is of interest to note, as well, the effect that the true penitent has upon heaven.

"There is joy in the presence of the angels of God over one sinner that repenteth" (Luke 15:7).

Now, if we were to ask the question, "What is repentance?" we would discover by a close investigation that there are many parts which combine to make up the whole. I should, however, like to draw your attention, not to each of these, but to a few of them.

First, then, confession. Confession is part of repentance; but before there can be confession, there must be conviction of sin, otherwise no need of confession is felt. There are many who, unaware of any sin, ask, "Why is there any need of confession?" There are others who, in a general way, would confess that they are sinners, yet would turn in anger if another individual dared accuse them in similar terms. The sense of sin and guilt is needed, otherwise there can be no true confession and the need for redemption and salvation is not seen.

Part of the preacher's duty is to seek to bring home this sense of sin and guilt. My suggestion to you is this—take the Ten Commandments, go over them one by one, and ask yourself if you have lived up to the demands that are thus made. Or I might make this other suggestion—let a man seek to give himself wholly to God, say, for one month, endeavour to keep his mind pure during that time, and if he is really honest with himself, he will become aware that there is need of cleansing within his own life. Or again, let it be noted that the unrest and dissatisfaction that attend so many lives may often be traced to sin that has never been repented of. Moreover, the Scriptures remind us very sternly that all have sinned.

If, perchance, anyone is able to say as they look into

the face of the Lord, " All these have I observed from my youth up," I feel confident that Christ would still point to one thing needful. For example, God's provision for man's need is through the sacrifice of Christ and His very definite word to every human soul is " He that believeth not is condemned already." It may be, then, that our confession should take the way of acknowledging that we have not believed in Christ as we should.

Secondly, contrition. This is another part of the content of repentance. Let me point out that there is what is theologically known as attrition as well as contrition, and these two require to be carefully distinguished. Attrition is simply sorrow because of the consequences of sin. Contrition is sorrow for sin. Sorrow that is aroused because the sin hurts another.

Now, not for a moment would I suggest that we despise attrition. It may in the end lead to contrition, for that is what took place in the case of the prodigal. Surrounded by all the evidences of his bankrupt condition, he began to meditate upon what he might have had. "How many hired servants of my father have bread enough and to spare? " But he went further than just sorrow because of the condition in which he found himself. He came to the place where he was prepared to realize that he had sinned against heaven and against the love of his father. " I have sinned against heaven and before thee, and I am no more worthy to be called thy son."

Sometimes what has been passed off as repentance has only been attrition. Men, by their own misdeeds, have led themselves into a position from which it would be difficult to extricate themselves without loss of honour. But when the danger passed, they no longer mourned over their sin—they were back participating in it.

But contrition comes near to the very heart of repentance, for it is true sorrow for sin. The sinner, aware of his sin in no small way, becomes truly sorry for that which hurts the heart of God. For example, a child who has transgressed some law of the home may feel sorrow because of the punishment that follows the transgression of that law, but not until the child has somehow discovered the hurt at the heart of the parent and sorrow because of that does it really know what true contrition is.

An apology to gain an immediate advantage must never on any account be considered as true contrition. The Lord turned and looked upon Peter. Peter went out and wept bitterly, and I believe in the weeping Peter we can see the true evidence of real contrition.

In the light of all this, it may be wise for us to pray, "Quicken my conscience till it feel the loathsomeness of sin."

And thirdly, there is a change of mind. That is, I understand, the meaning of the word repentance. In our natural condition we face away from God. To have a complete change of mind is to turn and face toward God. Naturally, our minds are at enmity to God. Repentance is to have a complete change of mind so that we are at one with God. Or to put it in the words of another, "Repentance really means agreeing with God upon everything."

The Catechism renders its definition thus: "Repentance unto life is a saving grace whereby a sinner, out of a true sense of his sin and apprehension of the mercy of God in Christ, doth with grief and hatred of his sin turn from it unto God with full purpose of and endeavour after new obedience."

The late Professor Mackintosh, in his book, "Forgiveness," sums up what we have been saying on this subject: "Repentance thus involves the three cardinal modes of being conscious—knowing, feeling, willing. Sin is recognized. It is disliked. It is disowned. Recognition of sin by itself is not repentance; it may be defiance. Nor is sorrow for sin repentance, if it be alone in the mind; it may be remorse or despair. Abandonment of sin, by itself, may be no more than prudence. The regenerating fact is all three as a unity, baptized in a sense of God's personal grace to the sinful."

Now, this question has to be answered. What have we done about this matter of repentance? There are some solemn words in Scripture. You remember our Lord on one occasion, speaking of His own generation, said, "It shall be more tolerable for Sodom and Gomorrah in the day of judgment than for you?" But we have had greater opportunities than those who lived in Christ's day, for we have lived in a Christian era with the Crucifixion, the Resurrection, and Pentecost all behind us; we have watched the growth of the Church, we have seen the enemy of souls beat with all his power against the living Church and not conquer it, and maybe we have known individuals whose experience obviously told of something outwith our ken. Surely, then, we are not stressing or misplacing the words of the Lord when we say, "It shall be more tolerable for Sodom and Gomorrah in the day of judgment than for you."

With this solemn warning sounding in our ears, let us turn to Him with true and full repentance, while there is yet time.

SEVEN

PRAYER

THERE are many types of prayer, but I want to speak about personal and private prayer. Prayer does not mean that we are always asking for things or seeking to get things; prayer can simply mean that in the same way as I want to be in the company of those I love, so I want to spend time alone with Him of whom the apostle said, "We love Him because He first loved us."

As I see it, prayer is getting in touch with God, and for the Christian man this is a most natural thing. Prayer is two-way. It means speaking to God, but it also means listening to God. It may be that the prayer life of many of us is taken up too much with talking to God, so that little time is left for Him to speak to us.

It is not necessary that one should be able to make long prayers, some of the prayers that have received the quickest answers have been short and direct. As, for example, when Peter in his need cried, "Lord, save me," and Jesus put forth his hand to keep him from sinking any further. And prayer is not for a special select few—

Prayer is the simplest form of speech that infant lips can try,
Prayer the sublimest strains that reach the Majesty on High.

I believe "that more things are wrought by prayer than this world dreams of."

I suggest that if you want to learn the art of prayer, you should seek to set aside a *quiet time*. My own opinion is that there is something to be said for making

38

it the same time each day where that is humanly possible. Make it a date just in the same way that you
would make an arrangement with any other, and let
nothing withhold you from keeping your appointment.

Then for the best use of that quiet time it is essential
that one find a *quiet place*. That is not always easy to
procure, and yet I have known many who have pro-
cured it by ingenious methods in order to keep tryst
with their Lord. One such comes to mind as I think
of a young Christian who lived in a home of two apart-
ments with a dividing corridor between. There was a
good-sized family, and so it was impossible for him to
secure a quiet place until all had retired, and then,
taking his chair into the corridor, he had a quiet time
alone with his Lord. To those serving in the Forces, the
difficulty of finding a quiet place for prayer is almost
insurmountable, yet not a few have found that the time
spent on guard at night can be well utilized for this
purpose.

But it is sometimes possible to secure a quiet time
and a quiet place, yet a third thing is essential, and that
is a *quiet heart,* which is not always easy to achieve.
How often we discover that in the place of prayer we
have little control over our thoughts as they are inclined to wander off over the general round of our
lives. These things we can, of course, bring and
mention before the Master, but they often control our
minds when we ought to control them.

Sometimes it is good to keep a book in which to
record on one side the different requests that we make
to God, and then on the other side to make an entry
when these are answered. A young fellow-student of
mine died suddenly during her university course.
Among her effects was found a little notebook. On
the one side were recorded her prayer requests and on

the other were noted any answers that had come. Looking over that little book, it was discovered that most of her definite prayers had been answered.

Let us remember this, that prayer has a very definite effect, first upon those who pray, and there is no man or woman who will make constant use of the place of prayer but will find that their spiritual experience is strengthened and their power over temptation is increased and their witness is made more vital. The Scriptures record of Moses as he came from the presence of God: "Moses wist not that the skin of his face shone." The influence of the man of prayer is powerful though he himself may not be aware of it.

And then it has its effect, secondly, upon those for whom prayer is made. That is one of the reasons, of course, why we pray, and I not only believe, but know it for a certainty, that prayer does change things in the lives of others.

I have recorded in my diary an incident in which I myself was the subject. Shortly after we landed in Normandy and the battle of Caen was in progress, I was walking across the orchard in which the tentage of our casualty clearing station had been pitched, when there came upon me a strange feeling of well-being, of exhilarance and buoyancy of spirit which was so unlike the sordid surroundings of wounded, mutilated and dying men. Another was accompanying me at the moment. This feeling was so marked that for a time I could not quite understand it, and then it seemed to dawn upon me what it might me. Turning to my companion, I asked him what day it was, and as he answered I looked at my watch and then I remembered that at that very moment there were a few praying souls who had gathered and were without a doubt praying for me in the church at home.

Then thirdly, prayer has an effect upon God. I say it reverently, your prayers and mine really have an effect upon God. Look at it this way. God, although all-powerful, has restricted Himself and possibly restricted Himself more than ever we realize. We know that He desires that much of His work should be done through human instrumentality, but He cannot use the human that has not yielded to Him. It is only as we pray that we come into the place of unity with Him, so that He can do through us all that he longs to do. Not until we pray can God do the work that He longs to do.

Or look at it this way. It seems to me that since the universe is governed by laws, the spiritual world, too, is governed by laws. Some law of evil cannot be controlled until some law of good is set free. That law for good cannot be set free until we pray, and just as the law of life in the human hand can affect the law of gravity by catching a cricket ball, so the law set in motion by our prayer may make of no effect the operation of the law of evil.

I suggest, therefore, that if we have never prayed before, we begin to pray to-day, and that if we have prayed, we pray still more so that God might be able to accomplish all His will for the world.

One last thought. Pray with an eye to the promises of God. Throughout the Scriptures God has made promises which we would do well to claim as our own. As we enter His presence we can make full claim to these promises and see them abundantly fulfilled in our lives and in the lives of others. If, by claiming the fulfilment of a promise from another, we receive the desired answer, how much more may we be assured of complete and detailed fulfilment when we make our claim to God.

Let us not minimize the worth and power of prayer. Its action is not limited to our immediate surroundings, for it releases power—divine power—with a world-wide influence.

> The weary ones had rest, the sad had joy
>   That day, and wondered " *How?* "
> A ploughman, singing at his work, had prayed,
>   " Lord, help them now."
>
> Away in foreign lands they wondered " *How?* "
>   Their simple word had power?
> At home, the Christians two or three had met
>   To pray an hour!
>
> Yes, we are always wondering, wondering " *How?* "
>   Because we do not see
> Someone, unknown perhaps, and far away,
>   On bended knee.

EIGHT

WHAT IS CHRISTIANITY?

I DO not suggest for one moment that I will either satisfy you or myself as I seek to answer this question, but I should like, if I can, to show you the direction in which I think the answer lies.

Have you thought much about this? Some have no doubt given it a fair amount of thought, some have thought superficially about it, some have thought fairly deeply and there are some who have found their answer and are satisfied. But even among Christians there are many who, in spite of all their thinking, have not yet fully answered this question.

I think we are agreed that it is a question of fair importance.

Now let us clear the way a little, for what I have to say is mainly taken up with pointing out what Christianity is *not*, and only towards the end will I suggest a possible answer to the question.

First, then, we must not confuse Christianity with civilization. Both are very closely connected. Wherever Christianity goes it always, without exception, carries the influence of civilization, but there were civilizations in existence long before Christianity was born. It is, however, true to say that where civilization goes it does not always bear Christian influences. A man can be a civilized person but not a Christian. A Christian, on the other hand, will sooner or later be a civilized person; and so it is perfectly evident that this distinction must be kept clearly in mind.

From my own point of view, it is much more important to Christianize than civilize, for the obvious reason that wherever Christianity is to be found, civilization follows. While wherever civilization arises, Christianity does not necessarily follow.

Secondly, we must not confuse Christianity with knowledge. Not for one moment would I suggest that you would confuse it with knowledge in a general way; for example, I do not think you would make the mistake of confusing Christianity with science, but I fear that a number of people equate knowledge about God and Christ and the Bible with Christianity.

Of course, Christianity does include knowledge about God and Christ and the Bible and the Church, but it is possible to have a knowledge of these and a fairly adequate knowledge, too, and yet not be a Christian. You see, my knowledge that Mohammed lived and died, together with whatever knowledge I may have of his life and of his work, and all that has been accomplished since his death does not make me a Mohammedan, and in the same way knowledge of God and Christ does not necessarily make me a Christian.

I read, for instance, somewhere that Mr. Gandhi admired Christ, that the hymnbook he used included, together with hymns addressed to Indian gods, such hymns as " Rock of Ages " and " When I survey the wondrous Cross "; but not for one moment would Mr. Gandhi have contended that he was a Christian. So we must be careful to distinguish between Christianity and knowledge of Christian things.

Thirdly, do not let us confuse Christianity with morality. Morality, of course, is included in Christianity, for Christianity without morality is impossible. A man who calls himself a Christian and is not moral is a hypocrite, but though there is this very close and vital connection between the two, let us remember that there were codes of ethics long before Christianity came into existence. Indeed the high moral code of the Jewish religion still holds a very honoured place in the world, and our own system of ethics is based upon it.

It is impossible to look at the lives of others without discovering that there have been moral heights attained even among what we might call pagan cults, and in this respect it may be well to remember that Jesus said, speaking of the Jewish law, " I am not come to destroy the law but to fulfil."

Fourthly, let us not confuse Christianity with organized religion. By organized religion I mean not one particular denomination, but every denomination as we see them to-day. Organized religion may fail. Christianity never will. And it is just here that grave concern is felt by some of us over a great deal of the teaching propagated in the name of organized religion in our land to-day, namely, that association with the

Church makes one a Christian. I have no desire to belittle church membership. Membership in the Christian Church is most important, but let it be said frankly and plainly that there are people who come to church, some of whom may have a more close association with the Church than others, and yet in the true sense of the term are not Christians. They have come to Church, but they have not come to God.

Now, having expressed all this in an effort to clear away any difficulties within our thought, we go back again to the question, "What, then, is Christianity?" There are many answers that might be given to the question. I have heard it answered in this way, that Christianity is a faith, a fight and a fellowship, and that might fairly comprehensively take in what Christianity is.

My purpose, however, is to narrow the answer to this question down to a single phrase or a single word. Christianity to me is a life. Indeed, it is the very life of Christ. He is the Alpha and the Omega, the beginning and the end, and everything in between. Christianity is life at its noblest, at its best. Christianity is eternal life started here and now. Christianity is Christ Himself within the individual who trusts. It is, as Paul would put it, "Christ in you." All of which may appear mysterious and mystical, and so it is, but it is nevertheless real, and when individuals really have a passionate desire to know what Christianity is, they shall find it for themselves in permitting Jesus Christ to possess their whole being and to allow Him to live out His life in and through them. And so the whole experience of life becomes changed. Henceforth it is not I but Christ. Henceforth the individual faces life's joys and life's sorrows, life's achievements and life's difficulties, not alone, but with Him, and if, peradventure, life should be looming dark and threatening for anyone, then Christianity can mean for all such what the writer of these words has found—

I cannot do it alone, the waves run fast and high,
  And the stars go out in the sky,
  And the storms beat loud and high,
But I know that we two shall win in the end,
    Jesus and I.

Coward and wayward and weak, I change with the changing sky,
  To-day so eager and bright, to-morrow too weak to try,
But He never gives in, so we two shall win,
    Jesus and I.

NINE

HAS GOD A DEFINITE PURPOSE FOR MY LIFE?

IF you should ask me that question and expect a definite answer, I would have no hesitation in saying—for I believe it with all my heart—that God HAS a definite purpose for each individual life.

I know that such a statement might arouse the antagonism of some and the disagreement of others, but my observance of life and my knowledge of the character of God leads me to make such a definite statement with no reservations whatever.

Most earthly parents plan for their children. They seek to direct them along the line of their own plans. They educate them towards that end. They introduce them to different people with this thought in view. If, then, the earthly parent initiates a plan for the life of his child, surely it is not going too far to say that the Divine Father plans the lives of His children.

A wise parent recognizes that in planning for his children he may make a mistake, but it is easy to see that God in this direction—indeed, in any direction—never makes a mistake.

"Do you mean, then," someone continues to ask, "that God has, as it were, a blue print for my life with everything great and small marked upon it?" and to that I answer an emphatic "Yes." Life can never be at its best for anyone until they are fulfilling that which God has purposed for them. This, too, must be remembered, that what we often describe as trivial things in life are not always so. The small and apparently inconsequent matter not only very often reveals our true character, but also decides in many cases the direction that our life shall take.

"You mean, then, that God is interested in my career?"—to which I reply, "Very much so." He is interested in whether you lead a life in the Services or a life as a civilian.

I have heard this story, and I am almost sure that it refers to the late J. G. Govan. One summer's day, lying on the hillside above the little village of Corrie in Arran, he was disturbed and distressed in soul, and as he lay there he was talking over the matter with God. As he did so, he was attracted to the little boats in the blue waters just beneath him. There was a little boat rowing about hither and thither. There was another little boat with a sail rigged, flitting backwards and forwards, obviously all out on pleasure bent; and then his eye was raised beyond that scene to the channel of the river down which a liner was moving. There it was, moving slowly, to him silently, and yet moving down the channel making for the open sea, and possibly right out to America. There was something majestic in its bearing, something purposeful in its effortless movement, and the divine question was put to him, "Has life to be for you like these little boats beneath, aimless, purposeless, purely on pleasure bent; or like the great liner out on the channel, steady, purposeful, with a definite aim in view?"

There are men whose lives are governed by this: let us eat and drink, for to-morrow we die. They are of no value, either to themselves or to others. Some other men are forceful, purposeful, but their purpose is a man-made goal, and often in their forcefulness they override others. The best life is that which seeks to fulfil the purpose of God; and if you think seriously for a moment you must come to this conclusion that the divine purpose, no matter how often it may appear to be otherwise, must be best.

God does not give to anyone the blue print of his life. It remains in His keeping. We are not permitted to see the end from the beginning, nor what is between these two extremities. And most of us, if not all of us, are really grateful for that. But the individual who steps out with a whole-hearted desire to follow out the divine plan is, without doubt, assured of guidance. He may simply trust, saying in the words of the hymn—

> I do not ask to see the distant scene,
> One step enough for me.

But trusting in that way—I can say it with all the authority that Scripture gives to me—that such a person will receive divine guidance. And if you would like some of the Scriptures that give me authority to say that, here they are: " In all thy ways acknowledge Him and He shall direct thy paths " (Prov. 3:6); " Commit thy way unto the Lord, trust also in Him, and He shall bring it to pass " (Psa. 37:5); " Thine ears shall hear a word behind thee saying: This is the way, walk ye in it " (Isa. 30:21).

Thus it is evident that anyone really desirous of having the divine purpose fulfilled in his life shall without doubt find his life directed and his way made plain, step by step.

Are you sufficiently interested to ask, "How can I start?" Let me bring to you the good news. We can start when we get right with God, who, as we all know, is willing to receive us almost at any time.

I have sometimes heard it said, "God can do nothing with a life like mine. Too much of it has already been wasted; it is dark and black and stained."

Let me tell you a story. There is a house in the Highlands that stands alone in its own grounds. In that house one day there was a party about to take place. The guests had begun to arrive when the hostess, to her horror, discovered that in her drawing-room some careless person had dropped a big spot of ink upon the wallpaper. She was distressed beyond words. What could she do? One of the guests who had already arrived heard of her dilemma. Coming into the drawing-room, he looked at it. It was an ugly blotch upon the otherwise beautiful room. Turning to his hostess, he said, "Don't trouble anything about it; I will see it all right"; and so, beginning upon it, out of that dirty, dark, disfiguring mark, this man drew a lovely picture. He was an artist of repute, and he put into it all the skill that he possessed. In a short time the whole thing was transformed.

Likewise, God takes up any life that appears wasted and dark with all the terrors that sin can bring upon it, so that out of that marred, disfigured life He may produce a worthy picture. And it is then, just then, that His purpose begins to be fulfilled in that life.

A story is told of the late Professor Henry Drummond. On one occasion, during one of his week-end preaching engagements, of which he had many, he was met at the station by his host. As they journeyed from the station to his host's home in their carriage, he was informed that the coachman, who was now getting advanced in years, had unfortunately begun to take a little more strong drink than was good for him, and it was incapacitating him for his work.

He had been a long and faithful servant, but his master had now come to the conclusion that he would require to dispense with his services unless he improved, and so he asked Professor Drummond to see if he could do anything with the coachman over the week-end.

As very often happens when one is seeking an opportunity to say a needed word, no opportunity arose in which Professor Drummond could get a single moment alone with the coachman. Monday morning came, and his host desired to accompany him to the station, but Drummond dissuaded him from entering the carriage, and he himself mounted beside the coachman. As they went along the road, conversation took place, and at one point Drummond said to the coachman, " Do your horses ever take fright? " " Yes," said the coachman, " Sometimes they do, but they are all right as long as the reins are in these hands of mine." And again Drummond asked, " Do they ever run away? " " Yes," said the coachman, " they may try it, but as long as the reins are in these hands of mine, everything is safe." With that they reached the station, and as they began to dismount, the old coachman threw the reins over the backs of his horses, and Drummond, in an instant, saw his chance and said, " Why not throw the reins of your life into the hands of God? ".

My dear men, that is the question I should like to ask you.

TEN

WHAT THINK YE OF CHRIST?
Matthew 22:42.

VARIOUS types of questions present themselves to us in life. One way in which they might be divided into different categories is this—questions that are unimportant, semi-important, and very important, according to the way in which the answer would affect the individual life.

This question, however, I suggest, falls outside any of these categories, for it is the most important question of all. Christ steps across the history of every man's life and asks, without egoism, "What do you think of Me?"

This question cannot be evaded; indifference will not alter the issue. For whether we answer it in words or not, our attitude to it nevertheless determines the nature of our character as also the nature of our destiny.

It sometimes surprises and distresses me that in our own country so many children do not have the opportunity of facing up to this question because the teaching concerning it is much neglected.

Not long ago, a child on holiday heard another little child in the same boarding house singing—

> Jesus loves me, this I know,
> For the Bible tells me so.

The first child raised the question with the second, "What is the Bible?" Something similar occurred in the evening when the child who had been singing knelt to say his prayers before being put to bed, and the other little soul began to question and asked, "What is a prayer?" There was not much chance of that child giving an intelligent answer, indeed, any answer, to this question, "What think ye of Christ?" When parents, who neglect to fulfil their responsibilities toward the Christian education of a child, come face to face with God, I do not know what answer they can possibly give.

But most of us do know what is meant when this question is asked, and most of us are aware that many books have been written in an effort to give an adequate answer. It is not possible to summarize all the thoughts that have been given concerning this question, but let me mention briefly three types of answers that have been given. It may even be that the line of thought suggested expresses your own opinion.

In the first place, there are those who think of Christ as a man. He is a historic figure whose life surpasses any other in moral grandeur. To any who would say the picture of Jesus in the Gospels is the figment of human imagination they would retort that not even a Shakespeare could imagine such a character and portray Him in any of his works. Those who look to Christ in this way admire the stainless purity of His moral character, praise the consistency of His life of good works, and while deprecating His early death, reverence Him as a martyr.

Secondly, there are those who would prescribe for Him priority of place among men of thought of every age. He is not to be compared with other thinkers as He far transcends them. His moral teaching, as depicted particularly in the Sermon on the Mount, stands unequalled in all history. He is One who always speaks with authority far beyond any human scribe, so that even those who were opposed to Him and who listened to Him had grudgingly to admit "Never man spake like this Man."

Thirdly, there are those who have conceived of Christ as a Leader—One whom most men would delight to follow. For all the attributes of leadership are to be found in Him, and He is ever worthy of unbroken confidence.

Now, Jesus Christ is certainly each of these. He is all three put together, and considerably more, for these do not adequately measure the life and character of Jesus Christ. They fail to take into consideration what was essentially His ministry—a ministry which was the very outcome of His character. "What think ye of Christ?" The Scriptures make answer: "He is the Saviour." Before His birth, these words were given by an angel visitor, "Thou shalt call His name Jesus, for He shall *save* His people from their sin" and He Himself said, "The Son of Man is to come to seek and to *save* that which was lost."

There is no religion of any standing that has not the word "salvation" within its vocabulary and the Christian religion would be completely bereft of any significance if the word were erased from its writings. Jesus Christ was a perfect Man, truly a moral ideal. He was a thinker whose words shall outlast time, He was a real leader of men, and before whom all shall yet bow, but any analysis of the character of Jesus Christ that ends there falls far short of a full or complete or final description of the character of Christ. Not until we begin to realize that He came to be the Saviour of men are we coming near to the true answer to this question.

The salvation of which Jesus Christ is the Author deals with the past, the present and the future.

When Christ becomes the Saviour of the individual,

the guilty past is dealt with and the penalty for sin is taken away, the individual stands in that moment saved. " There is therefore now no condemnation to them who are in Christ Jesus."

But its reference is also to the present, for the soul who knows Him as Saviour discovers that moment by moment, day by day, as he depends upon His Saviour, there is power to overcome—power to overcome temptation, power to say " No " to sin—" He breaks the power of cancelled sin, He sets the prisoner free."

But the salvation which Christ brings also has a reference to the future—saved yesterday, being saved to-day, the soul has confidence in His word that He will continue to save in the days that lie ahead, and, indeed, the salvation is never fully completed until the day when He has promised to present us faultless before the presence of His glory with exceeding great joy. So in the end we shall be saved from the very presence of sin. " Who delivered us from so great a death and doth deliver. In whom we trust that He will yet deliver us " (2 Cor. 1 : 10).

" What think ye of Christ? " Some might even answer, " He is a Saviour," giving Him a place among many others. Some might answer to the same question, " He is THE Saviour," the only One without any rival whatever. Yet it is possible to believe that Christ is THE Saviour of the world without it having any effect whatever upon the individual life, but there are many who can say as an answer to this question, " He is MY Saviour," and in that answer they make articulate an experience in which they have found that Christ has come near to them and though they do not deserve it He has, by His grace, saved them.

I read a short time ago in one of our magazines an

article by Rear-Admiral G. B. Allan, R.N., in which he stated, " Christ is my Saviour. This is not simply a Sunday-school expression."

You might well turn and ask me, " What do YOU think of Christ? " and all that I could say is this: " Words fail to express not only what I think of Christ but what I know of Him, but I certainly could truthfully say He is MY Saviour."

You may remember Jesus speaking to His disciples one day and asking this question, "Whom do men say that I am? " and after they had given various replies He looked at them, it seems to me, straight in the eyes and said, not unkindly, " Whom say *ye* that I am? " That is just His other way of asking this same question, and the answer, do not forget, determines the type of life that you are going to live here and the shape of your destiny in the hereafter.

ELEVEN

WILT THOU BE MADE WHOLE?
John 5:6.

BETHESDA, the name of the pool in the incident before us, according to some, means "House of Mercy." If so, the name is probably due to the function of the place. I think we can take it that something really took place at that pool, for no story without substance would have been able to continue with credence against the cold necessity of these people, for there were a number who were lying around waiting for healing.

But our attention is focused on one man. A certain man was there who had been an invalid for thirty-eight years. "Wilt thou be made whole?" he was startled to hear. That would indeed be a heartless question to address to any sufferer and so arouse a measure of hope within his breast unless there was something more than hope behind it.

And the story reveals that there was a great deal more behind it.

Look, then, in the first place at the man and his need. He recognized that there was something wrong, and so was there for healing. We might not have known that there was any connection between his sin and his physical disability had not our Lord given us the clue in verse 14: "Behold, thou art made whole, sin no more lest a worse thing come unto thee." Our Lord, however, knew about that connection. Jesus, in His approach to the man endorsed what the man already knew, namely, that he needed healing.

Note that the sufferer had put his trust in other things for healing, but each had failed. Firstly, he had trusted in the remarkable phenomenon of the pool, whatever it was. From what he says, he had seen it at work, but he had not been able to avail himself of its powers.

Secondly, he had trusted in himself, but any power that he possessed was insufficient to enable him to reach the pool before someone more able than himself had entered into it.

And thirdly, he had trusted in others, but when he needed them most they had failed him. He had no one to help him—not a soul was there who would give him the helping hand that he needed and put him into the pool. He was friendless, forsaken by all who had once called him friend.

When at the end of his resources, realizing possibly that his case was now hopeless, maybe his mind turning Godwards with real humility, Jesus came near. How great is the mercy and kindness and grace of our Lord! And seeing the man in his need, and realizing that he had faith to be healed, he said, "Rise, take up thy bed and walk," and in that moment the man's sin was dealt with, and his bodily health was restored.

In the second place, let us think of ourselves and our need. Have we ever heard the Master addressing these words to us, "Wilt thou be made whole?" It is not for nothing that He asks such a question. Does it startle someone into a recognition of a need of which they were not aware? Not a few men, when called up for medical examination, were made aware for the first time of a physical weakness. The tragedy of many is that they they are not aware of any spiritual malady that requires the word of authority from the Master.

Or does this question, "Wilt thou be made whole?" addressed to us, endorse what has been gradually borne in upon us, that we are ill with a grievous malady? Then this question need not only arouse hope within our breast—it can be a forerunner of the words, "Rise, take up thy bed and walk."

According to the story, there are definite types of people in this condition—there were those who were blind. That truly represents the spiritual condition of some. It actually is the condition of the unregenerate heart. Make no mistake about it, anyone who has not come to know Jesus Christ for himself cannot see in a spiritual sense—that to me is the only explanation of the conduct of many people who like to call themselves Christians. Oh, the tragedy of it! Blind, and not aware of it. Oh, that I could bring them to Christ or

Christ to them for "something lives in every hue
Christless eyes have never seen."

And then there were folks halt. That simply means
limped—they limped, they hirpled along. Does that
not represent the Christian soul that is so easily tripped
up? I wonder how many Christians are living that
type of life? Some sin—temper, jealousy, or that they
are easily put out, walking the Christian life in a halting
manner, when they could be running with strong and
steady steps. "Wilt thou be made whole?" says Jesus.

Then there were those who were withered—withered
just simply means dried up. That is not only an
ancient story—it is a modern one in the spiritual sense.
Some gifts are atrophied through lack of use. The
capacity to sing, the power to do some individual work
for the Master, the conscience without sensitiveness—
"Wilt thou be made whole?"

And so, in the third place, there is the remedy for
all this. We find it in the words of the Master, "Rise."
That is, do at the Master's command what before you
could not do in your own strength: "Take up thy bed."
That surely means that no provision should be made
for a relapse. How often we make that mistake! To
put it in other words, it just simply means "burn your
boats." "Walk" may be expressed thus: "Don't
expect to be carried." The Lord has imparted to us life
and health in order that we each may walk.

Later on Jesus found this man in the temple giving
thanks for the blessing he had received. He was in the
right place.

Surely if this incident has a message for any of us,
we want to say: —

> Saviour, I yield, long to be healed,
>   Praying Thee now to receive me,
> Searching my heart, bid to depart,
>   Everything there that would grieve Thee.

TWELVE

WILL A MAN ROB GOD?
Malachi 3:8.

A SUNDAY-SCHOOL teacher some years ago was teaching his class of young children, and in order to make the lesson graphic, he began by asking this question, " Can you think of anyone so wicked as to rob your parents? " Without any hesitation the reply from the majority of the class was, "Oh, yes."

Then he continued, " Do you think there is anyone so wicked as to rob your minister? " For a moment there was hesitancy, but before long they had all come round to the position where they were perfectly sure that it was possible that someone could rob their minister.

He continued with this further question, and he put all the meaning he could into the tone of his voice, " Do you think there is anyone who would be so wicked as to rob the Queen? " That puzzled them for a moment, and then one little soul took courage and rose to her feet and said, " Yes, I think there is some one who would be wicked enough to rob the Queen."

This final question he then put to them, and here again he sought to bring the full play of his personality into it as he asked, " Do you think there is anyone so wicked as to rob GOD? " There was silence for a moment or two and then the unanimous answer of the whole class was " NO." These young children could not think that anyone would be so wicked as to rob God. Yet that is the charge that God makes in this

Scripture: " Ye have robbed Me," He says. It is not a statement that is modified in any way. Rather it is the definite answer which God makes to His own question, " Will a man rob God? "

Is there no substance in the charge that God makes? No one who has any sure knowledge of himself can deny that there is. On the occasion when God made this charge, He answered the astonished question of the people, "Wherein have we robbed Thee? " by saying, " In tithes and offerings," but I should like to show that the charge is more serious than that.

We may see the true standpoint if we put it in the form of a question, "How many of us have, by an irrevocable act of our will, returned our lives to God? " You will, of course, remember that we are God's. It is He who has created us, and so we are the creatures of His creation. We are thus His by this right. But, moreover, we are His twice over, for, in addition to being creatures of His creation, we are the redeemed of His redemption. He has purchased us back at a price of the life of His Son.

Let me tell this well-worn story, for it illustrates our point very well.

A little lad had made a boat with his own hands. It was all the more precious because he had made it, and it was a great thrill to see it sail upon the water. But one day it was taken beyond his reach as he sailed it and was carried out to sea. What a tragedy to the little heart! What sorrow in such a loss! Some time later, looking in a toyshop window, he was surprised as he noticed with delight that there was a little boat displayed. He had only to look at it once to recognize it as his own.

Immediately he entered the shop and demanded that the boat be given to him, as it was his by right since he had made it with his own hands, but he came out of the shop disconsolate. The shopkeeper refused to give it to him. He would not accept the little lad's story. In the course of the discussion that ensued, the boy discovered that the boat could be purchased at the price of a shilling, but the shilling was beyond his means.

Returning home with tear-stained face, he explained with sobs all about his boat, and the wise parents gave him the shilling that he required. So, with hurrying feet, he returned to the shop, paid his shilling, received his boat, and, hugging it as he went out, he was heard to say, "My own wee boat, I made you and I have bought you—twice over you belong to me."

And that is a true picture of our position before God. God made us. We are His by creation, but we were lost to Him because of sin, and so He purchased us back at the price of His own Son.

Yet in spite of this fact that twice over we belong to God, we can still withhold ourselves from Him, for He has given us free will, and He may still be saying to us to-day, "Ye have robbed Me—robbed Me of that which is really Mine because you are wilfully withholding yourself from Me."

Does this in any degree come near to a true picture of our relationship with God? If it is, it is a sad reflection upon the gratitude of human nature. We would deplore such conduct exhibited in any human relationship, yet we ourselves may be guilty of such conduct with God.

Now, there is much that God longs to do among men, but just cannot because He has limited Himself in arranging that much of His work upon the earth should be accomplished through human agency. He longs to do this work, and He longs to do it through

us, but He will not force us into service. He desires
that we might willingly return ourselves to Him that
He might direct us in His work.

There is a story told of a serious railway accident.
The engine of the train had fallen on its side, and the
driver of the engine had been pinned by the legs
underneath it. It so happened that a famous surgeon
was on the train, and he came and examined the injured
man. After his examination those around asked the
surgeon, " Can you do anything to save his life? " The
answer that he gave was this: " Yes, if I had my
instruments." But unfortunately he was without his
instruments.

As I look out into the world to-day and see it in its
need—and how extensive is that need!—I feel like
praying thus: " Oh, God, could you save the world
from its troubles and sorrows and sin? " and I feel
I hear Him saying, " Yes, if I had My instruments."
When I think of the Church and the Church's need,
and the individual member within the Church and
his need, I feel like saying to God, " Oh, God, could
you send revival? " and I think I hear Him saying,
" Yes, if I had My instruments."

And you and I are His instruments, and He needs
us. In the light of all this pressing need, shall we refuse
Him our lives any longer?

God grant that to-day our response may be that
our lives with all their possessions be returned to Him
in a glad and willing surrender, and hear Him say,
" Thou art Mine."

THIRTEEN

"THOU ART SIMON—THOU SHALT BE"
John 1:42.

"I WILL MAKE YOU"
Matthew 4:19.

I T is not likely that Jesus and Simon had met before this incident recorded in the first chapter of John's Gospel, so it must have come as a tremendous shock to Simon to hear words from this stranger which laid his own soul bare, for I feel sure that Jesus that day did make known to Simon the very condition of his heart. In that moment, it seems to me, Simon realized that before him stood One who knew the very deepest secrets of his heart, and Simon was startled by such a revelation, for it meant that nothing could be hidden from this Jesus.

"He knew what was in man." What John stated in these words concerning Jesus was amply shown to Simon that day. Thus, when Jesus said, "Thou art," there was no question as to the accuracy of his diagnosis of Simon's condition.

What was Simon like? I feel sure that you and I would have found Simon a good companion. We would, while recognizing his limitations, have loved him, for he was always anxious to help and never at any time disobliging. His anxiety to be of assistance to others was such that there were times that he overstepped what he could possibly accomplish, and so he was not always able to fulfil all the promises he made. This almost grew into a fault, for no matter how much he was loved, it became apparent that he could not always be trusted simply because of his inability to keep all the promises he made.

From the first, Jesus knew this weakness of Simon, and Simon, as he stood before the Master that day, recognized that Christ knew this about him. Some have described Simon's nature with such descriptive words as "shifting sands," and that term is certainly not inappropriate. Nothing of lasting value could be built on such a foundation. But Jesus did not reveal Simon's weakness to him to taunt him with it, but to point him to a better experience and to a different type of character, and that is shown in the words, "Thou shalt be."

Now, the Master is eternally the same. He has not quitted the scene of human experience, but to-day still looks straight into the eyes of each individual and says, "Thou art," and if we know anything about ourselves we are aware that there is no mistake in the delineation of our character which He makes.

What might then be the truth about us? This at least, "Thou art less than you would be." Each of us is conscious that we fall far short of the type of life that in our best moments we long to live. We see the ideal which we fain would achieve, but which, no matter how much we try, we fail to reach. Sometimes because of our failures we are inclined to give up in despair. "Thou art less than you would be."

And more, "Thou art less than you *could* be." Surely we are each conscious, too, of this—that we have not attained to the stage in the development of our character that might be expected of us. Think of all the privileges in which we have shared. Can we honestly say that we have used these to the best advantage? A great measure of responsibility lies at our own door for the lack of development in Christian character. Jesus Christ looks into your eyes and mine and says, "Thou art less than you could be," and we are wise if we pay heed to what He says.

Simon that day was not left merely with this unflattering self-portrait. Jesus had a more gracious word to say to him. He had not appeared to leave him in the condition in which He had found him, so there is real hope in the words which he addressed to him, "Thou shalt be Cephas."

To grasp the full significance of that promise made to Simon is to understand at the same time something of the outstanding nature of the work which the Master came to do. "Cephas" is the Hebrew word for "rock" or "stone," just as Peter is the Greek word meaning the same thing. The promise, then, given to Simon by the Master was a complete change of character that would be as radical as the change from sand to rock. What visions were pictured in Simon's mind by this revelation of himself and the promise made to him one could only guess, but it must have put new heart into him if at the same time doubts and misgivings would arise as to the possibility of fulfilment in such a character as his.

Let us not forget our Lord is saying the same thing to-day. "Thou shalt be." As He has spoken to us and reminded us of our weakness, He has also given this word of sure promise which reminds us of the possibilities that lie within us. A change of nature such as He alone can effect is promised so that failures become successes and ideals, once seen, have a real chance of becoming realities. An illustration of this truth can be taken from a geological lesson to which I once listened. Sandstone with which we have built some of the greatest structures, is formed in the bed of a river or the floor of the sea. The sand sinks to the bottom, and with each successive tide a further layer of sand is laid. This, together with other ingredients and something to combine the whole, ultimately over a long period becomes solid rock—sand becomes rock.

And this is the message of this incident. From that which is unreliable there shall arise that which is dependable. Peter will no longer have a nature that can be likened to shifting sands, but a nature that is dependable as rock. In other words, a character which can be trusted. And so, in Peter, there is the material which can act as the foundation upon which to build a secure structure or, in other words, there is substance upon which others can depend, and you remember one day Jesus did say to Simon, realizing that the change had almost taken place, " Thou art Peter—thou art rock."

Now, when to-day the Master says to us, " Thou shalt be," does such a promise picture to us much that we desire? We may be tempted to say that it presents a vision which only mocks us, as it seems completely unattainable. This is the prospect that lies before us —assured victory where there has been constant defeat; success where before we could only expect failure; sin overcome to which in the past we so easily fell; equal to tasks that before were impossible; standing for right amid the forces of evil.

It seems to me that Simon that day looked up wistfully into the Lord's face and showed a yearning for the fulfilment of the promise within his life. It may be that, like us to-day, he showed perplexity as to how it might all be fulfilled, but we can rest assured that when Christ makes a promise to any man, He is capable of fulfilling it.

At a later date in Simon's history, Jesus said to him,

" I will make you." There lies the secret of Christian success at any time. Human endeavour may not be wholly unavailing, but it is powerless to accomplish what, in our best moments, we desire—only Christ can do this for us, and He has promised to do it. " I will make you." Surely such words come with real cheer to any who have found their need and who have also found their impotence to meet that need.

Look at the later life of Peter. What a tower of strength He was to the early Church. You cannot follow Peter's life then without realizing that Christ's promise was fulfilled to him in a most remarkable way. True, he had his occasions of failure, but ultimately he became the very leader upon whom so many depended for direction and guidance.

In this respect, the days of miracles are not past. God, through Christ, can make any of us stalwart for the faith. He can fulfil every promise He makes to us, " Thou art now, but thou shalt be, because I will make you."

Mary Slessor, that great Scottish missionary, when a young woman in Dundee, was afraid of cattle passing in the street, and would always take refuge when she happened to meet any. Yet when called to Africa by God, she often stood alone, the only white woman around for hundreds of miles, representing her own Government as well as her Lord and Master. No doubt if anyone had said to Mary Slessor in her early days that she would one day stand alone in this way, she would have rejected any such thought. And her case might well be summed up in these words, as if they came from the lips of the Master, " Mary, thou art, but I will make you, and thou shalt be."

Now, this is not simply a theological statement of what might have taken place, but a definite message for you and me to-day. It has a very definite practical and experimental value. What are you going to make of it? Says Christ, "I will make you," but He will not force Himself upon us. He asks for permission to begin this gracious ministry in our hearts now. We can say that we will have nothing to do with Him, or we may say that we are now ready for Him to begin His gracious work in our lives.

Which is it to be?

FOURTEEN

FOLLOW ME—AND HE AROSE AND FOLLOWED HIM

Mark 2:14.

THIS is the challenging call which Jesus Christ makes to every man who has heard the Gospel message. It is a challenge that we do well to accept, for even if in response to it we discover that we are led through paths of life that we would never have chosen for ourselves, we shall nevertheless come to realize that it was all for our own good as we followed Him.

There are some men who would like to follow Jesus Christ, but they are not prepared to make the decision that is necessary and to turn their backs upon the old life. They are like some of the men of Christ's day. They say, "Lord, let me first go and bid them farewell who are at home." Often, it has to be recorded, many actually never leave their old associates and companions and come out boldly for Jesus Christ.

Let there be no mistake about it, the question of decision is important. It is all very well to think of Christ as someone worthy to follow, someone with whom you would be glad to be associated, but that never makes anyone a disciple of His.

Whether Matthew made his decision to follow Jesus Christ that day on the spur of the moment immediately he heard His voice or slowly made the decision having watched Christ on previous occasions, I do not know, but I know this, that for Matthew it was a most courageous thing to do. For in an instant Matthew's business and Matthew's money were left. He made this momentous decision and for ever after his life was lived in an entirely different way. Each subsequent reference to Matthew shows that he held to his decision to follow Christ.

It seems to me that there are many who have watched Jesus Christ, sometimes as they have seen Him in the life of others, and have desired to follow Him, but how few make the necessary decision! Surely it is strange that they should evade this main issue, for in other matters such as business and sport and worldly attainment they are so keen.

When Mary Collett was lying dying and John Inglesant, her great friend, had come to see her, this was a question that she put to him: "Will you serve your heavenly Master as well as you have served your King?"

We have all heard, and some of us have seen, the fanaticism of Nazi youth. Would it not be great if that same allegiance and loyalty could be given to Jesus Christ? A young Nazi was admitted fairly seriously wounded, into a casualty clearing station. He had been shot with a Sten gun bullet which had narrowly missed his heart. He was only seventeen, but he was a strong fanatical Nazi. Lying in bed, his only regret was that the bullet had not gone through his heart so that he might have died for his Fuehrer. Yes, men are willing to go to any length for worldly causes, but how few are willing to follow Christ wherever He leads!

" Jesus hath now many lovers of His heavenly kingdom, but few bearers of His cross. He hath many desirous of consolation, but few of tribulation. He findeth many companions of His table, but few of His abstinence. All desire to rejoice with Him, few are willing to endure anything for Him or with Him. Many follow Jesus into the breaking of bread, but few to the drinking of the cup of His Passion. Many reverence His miracles, few follow the ignominy of His Cross."

So said Thomas à Kempis.

Yet there is another side to all this. In the Acts of the Apostles we read of men who have hazarded their lives for the sake of the Gospel, and the Church's history all down the ages is a glorious record of men and women of valour who never counted their lives dear if only they could be all that Jesus Christ desired they should be.

I remember listening to a business man of very good standing tell that early in his life as a young Christian, he felt the call of Christ and, entering his office one morning a little bit troubled in spirit as to what his Lord was demanding of him, he stood a little while in prayer before he opened his desk. Taking the keys from his pocket, he laid them upon the top of the desk and said, "Lord, there are the keys, and if it is Thy desire I will leave everything this day and go out and follow Thee wheresoever Thou wilt lead." But Christ had other work for him to do, and he is still an outstanding business man and at the same time doing a wonderful work for God.

How I long that men would follow Jesus Christ with the same passion, enthusiasm and abandon as they prosecute their business or professional careers.

Wouldn't it be grand to hear a chorus sung by men from all sections of society: "Tho' he lead me thro' the fire, I'll go with him all the way"?

If you were to enter politics to-day as a member of any party, that party would expect you to vote in accordance with the policy of the party. And when Jesus Christ calls any man to follow Him, the response He demands is whole-hearted allegiance to His person and to His message with no reservations whatever.

This is what He expects from each of us now. Shall we, then, captivated by Him, make, at this moment, a definite, irrevocable decision, come what may, to follow Him right to the end of life's day?

> I heard the call, "Come, follow"; that was all;
> Earth's joys grew dim, my soul went after Him.
> I rose and followed—that was all:
> Will you not follow when you hear His call?

FIFTEEN

"HE MAKETH THE DEAF TO HEAR"

Mark 7:37.

HERE is the story of a man completely deaf and with an impediment in his speech. His friends brought him to Jesus and in response to their request Jesus gave to him perfect hearing and unbroken speech. Remember this, Christ never performed miracles simply to attract attention to Himself, nor, to my mind, did He perform them simply to help those upon whom the miracle was performed. Each instance of physical healing definitely points to a spiritual truth.

This, then, is one aspect of the message to be gathered from this story. In order that we might know that Jesus Christ came to give spiritual hearing to the spiritually deaf, this man was made whole.

Some years ago, on returning after a period of absence to my home, which was on the edge of the countryside, my father and I took a walk together along a country road. It was a beautiful April day, the sun shone brilliantly, the new life of spring was abundantly evident, and to me, who had returned after some time in the city, the air was strangely fragrant. As we walked we talked, and then, suddenly stopping in his step, my father turned to me and said, "Don't you hear it?" to which I replied, "Hear what?" "Listen," he said, and then to my unaccustomed ear came the chirp of a bird which by his attuned ear was heard immediately the bird had begun its tuneful song. He then began to explain that this was a bird uncommon in the district, and continued to tell me a great deal more about it.

The point to be noted from this incident is that my father, interested in country life and bird life in particular, had ears to hear, while I, unconcerned by all that was taking place around, had ears but could not hear.

The same truth can be observed in the realm of music. There are some people who never seem to hear music at all. Some can chatter away while the best of music is being played to them, as if it found no response in their souls, while others, sitting with attuned ears, feel it a perfect sacrilege to talk while such music is being played.

And all that leads me on to this: There is such a thing as spiritual deafness. One aspect of Christ's mission can be summed up in these words, "He maketh the deaf to hear," or, to put it in the phrase of the prophet Isaiah, "The ears of the deaf shall be unstopped" (Isa. 35:5).

God, since the time that He began to speak to man, has never ceased to speak. He speaks in many ways and in various voices. He sometimes speaks through friendships, through providences, through the gentle pleadings of His Spirit, and at other times through the sorrows and disappointments and the thunderings of life. But unless the ear has been attuned, these efforts on the divine part to make us listen to Him pass unheard. Says Bishop Westcott in his commentary of John's Gospel, "Like all spiritual things, this voice required preparedness in the organ to which it was addressed."

Now, this spiritual deafness is accentuated in different ways. First, we can become so used to His Voice as not to hear. In the same way as it is possible to sleep through an alarum clock even although on the first few occasions of its use we might have been startled beyond words.

And secondly, it is possible to be so busily engaged in other quite legitimate pursuits of life so that we have no time to listen to the Divine Voice.

Thirdly, this deafness may be accentuated by complete unconcern.

You remember the story told by John, in which Jesus had made a blind man to see. Brought before the Jews, he explained to them how it happened, but they refused to understand. Later on, he was again before the same authorities, and on this occasion the man began to revile them and to say, speaking of the former occasion, "You would not hear, wherefore would you hear it again." It is possible to listen to words and not to understand what has been said. And yet here is the message of the Gospel, no matter how deaf we may be to all the various cadences of the Divine Voice so that we live in our own made world oblivious to what He is saying to us, this deafness may be cured. Jesus Christ came to make the deaf to hear—in other words to restore to those who will allow Him spiritual hearing.

Think of this man of the story for a moment. Somehow he had become aware of his need. What that need fully was I do not think he could understand. Others seemed to possess something which he did not possess. What it was he was not quite sure, but he knew that it was something of extreme value.

When Christ had given to him his hearing then he understood in a way that it was impossible for him to know before. Think of the new experience into which he entered. He heard birds singing—that was something new. He heard music. There were words of friendship and love all sounding new and fresh and sweet to him. What a change Christ had made!

You remember Paul's experience on the Damascus road. He heard Christ speaking to him and understood what the Lord was saying. But the others standing around did not understand. In that moment, I am of the opinion, Saul's ears were opened to hear the Divine Voice and from that day forth he never ceased to listen to that Divine Voice.

Writing to the Corinthians, he tells us that on one occasion he heard words unspeakable that he could never have appreciated had he not experienced the miracle of hearing brought to deaf spiritual ears.

All around us just now there is music and speech in the air. We would not have believed it in days gone past, and in our natural state we cannot hear it, but put a wireless set there, tune it in, and you listen and hear what otherwise could not have been heard. And so, too, must the individual have his set, as it were, tuned to the Divine Voice so that he might constantly hear what God the Lord has to say. Isaiah, speaking again, says, " In that day shall the deaf hear the words of the book " (Isa. 29:18). It is through the Bible that God often speaks. It is possible to read it and not to hear His Voice, but it is possible to read it and to hear His Voice and in order that we might enjoy the wonder of His message to us, Christ came to give hearing to deaf ears. Bishop Westcott again states the case thus: "The apprehension of a Divine Voice depends upon man's capacity for hearing."

Unless we have this we shall miss the word of guidance which is promised in a word like this, " Thine ears shall hear a word behind thee saying, This is the way, walk ye in it, when ye turn to the right hand and when ye turn to the left " (Isa. 30:21). So also would we miss the words of pardon, of comfort and consolation, of strength and command, if we did not possess the ear that hears.

My closing word is a message addressed to Christian people. The story tells us that this man's friends brought him and besought Jesus on his behalf. Might I ask this question, "How often do we bring such needy souls to Jesus?" We can bring them at least in prayer, and sometimes, enabled by His grace, we may bring them in actual fact to Him.

SIXTEEN

THE VALUE OF RELIGIOUS EXPERIENCE

WILLIAM JAMES has a book which he entitles "Varieties of Religious Experience." That is a true statement, for there are many kinds of experience, all of which might be termed religious. Moses, you may remember, had a religious experience while he tended the flocks of his father-in-law. While there, he noticed one day a bush which was set on fire, but as he looked, the bush itself was not consumed, and when he drew near to behold this amazing sight he heard a voice from the midst of the bush saying, "Take off thy shoes from off thy feet, for the place whereon thou standest is holy ground." And that meant for Moses a realization that God was speaking to him, interested in him, and had something for him to do.

Saul had a religious experience on the Damascus road. There, having been struck to the earth, he realized that Jesus, the risen Christ, was speaking to him, and from that day Saul's whole life was completely turned about and completely reorganized.

For the sake of clarity, let us narrow our subject to Christian experience, and for the sake of definiteness I should like to narrow it even further to what I might term the initial Christian experience. In other words, what has often been termed conversion.

When God speaks in this very definite way to a man and changes the whole direction of his life, certain things take place.

First, a man can never be the same again. Like Saul, he becomes a Christian in an out-and-out way, thus having accepted the challenge that is presented to him, and he refuses to return to the old life, knowing that the life into which he has entered is God-given and God-controlled, with a God-inspired vision to follow.

Moses' experience I should like to consider as Christian experience, for it is an Old Testament counterpart of this New Testament characteristic; the burning bush incident meant for him that the whole tenor of his life was changed and the Damascus road incident meant for Saul a reorganization of his thinking and of his activity. This produced so outstanding a transformation that no one could be deceived as to what had taken place.

Here is an up-to-date story of the same thing. I was reading an article in "Practical Christianity," which is the organ of the Officers' Christian Union, written by Lt.-Col. D. C. D. Munro, D.S.O., M.C., D.C.M.

In his article he states that he was a lifetime in the Army. His whole background was associated with keen Christian people, but for most of his life he had not become one of them. However, there came a time when he wanted to be like them, and as that desire deepened, there was much heart searching. One day, in a street in London, he prayed, "Lord Jesus, come into my heart and keep me from sin," and the Lord answered his prayer and from that day he was a changed man.

The second thing is that a man cannot forget it. Take the illustration of Moses again. It is impossible to read through his life without realizing that that experience of his had an effect upon his whole life and on the different phases of it. And when he came to the end of his day, he still remembered that early meeting with God and spoke of the Lord who appeared to him in the midst of the bush: and someone, writing of Saul, who, of course, became Paul, says that the secret of St. Paul's freshness was that he never got over his conversion.

Yes, one of the wonders of the individual's initial Christian experience is that it just cannot be forgotten. Oh, it may be that it is crowded out for a little while, but sooner or later it is brought back to memory and the challenge that it brought is once more forced to the individual's notice.

It is true, of course, that it is not wise to be always harping back to the beginning of things. There are too many Christians who never seem to have made any progress beyond that of which they sing in the words:

> Oh, happy day that fixed my choice
> On Thee, my Saviour and my God.

Nevertheless, like the Psalmist who said, "He brought me up also out of a horrible pit," the very gratitude of the Christian heart keeps him in remembrance of that early experience as he says, thinking of some forlorn soul, "There go I, but for the grace of God."

> Oh, the love that drew salvation's plan,
> Oh, the grace that brought it down to man.

Thirdly, it carries conviction.

In a court of law what is required is not hear say evidence, but the evidence of an eye-witness. That is the evidence that always carries most weight. And to the question, " What do you know about it? " speaking of Christian experience, the man who has had experience can reply, " I was there when it happened, so I ought to know." There is nothing like being sure, and when the individual knows without any shadow of a doubt of his experience of the living Christ, he just cannot be moved. The man who declared with emphasis, "Once I was blind, now I see," was unconcerned about what other people thought of him or even about any scientific investigation that others might want to make of the cure. This new experience of his carried with it a conviction that nothing shattered.

Now, when a man, in this way, is sure, his assurance in a measure becomes contagious, and so it is passed on to others. There are few converts ever made by a person who is not too sure, whose speech is full of uncertainties and maybe's and perhaps, but when a man, sure of what he himself has experienced, declares to another without hesitancy what he himself knows, it bears weight in the mind of his hearers.

All of us, without exception, have been acquainted with those who have had such initial cataclysmic Christian experiences. And it may be that we are asking the question, "How may be enter into this? "

Allow me then to say, first, that the initiative is on the divine side. By that I mean that God desires to come into vital relationship with every human soul, and in order that that might be accomplished, He sent Jesus Christ into the world to make possible for man the way back to God—the way that had been closed because of sin and now Christ stands and says, "I am the Way." Through Him we have direct access to God when we come by faith.

And secondly, there must be the human response. As I have said, God has shown his interest in man by sending Christ. His interest is further exhibited in the way he constantly seeks to bring to man's notice His desire that every human should enjoy His best, but in order that it might be enjoyed, the human must respond. While I move around among you, I discover that many are rather in agreement with what I would say in an address like this, and in a measure realize that the onus of responsibility is now upon them, but they are not prepared to take the step. I would like to plead with you to allow no personal desire or worldly thought to keep you back from making that decision that would bring you to a real living experience of God in Jesus Christ.

Someone said, "What is wrong with us is that we are not men enough to be Christians." Oh that God, by His Holy Spirit, would give you the grace to be men enough to make a definite, irrevocable decision to come to Him!

SEVENTEEN

"WAIT ON THE LORD; BE OF GOOD COURAGE AND HE SHALL STRENGTHEN THINE HEART. WAIT, I SAY, ON THE LORD"

Psalm 27:14.

THE word "wait" is twice repeated within this text, and the meaning of the whole verse seems to be that the secret of new strength in the midst of all that would tend to weaken, is waiting upon God. Isaiah endorses what the Psalmist here says, for you remember Isaiah said, "They that wait upon the Lord shall renew their strength." And to say the same thing in other words, we might quote the psalm which says, "In quietness and in confidence shall be your strength."

"Wait" simply means to get alone with God. To meditate in His presence. To await His commands and fulfil His wishes. That, no doubt, many humans find difficult. It is not something that comes naturally to them, and yet if we would know the strength of which both psalmist and prophet speak, this attitude of waiting must surely be cultivated.

Before we can come, however, there must be some belief in God and some experience of Him. "Him that cometh to God must believe that He is, and that He is the rewarder of them that diligently seek Him."

Now, let us return to the thought of the psalm. In what circumstances was it written? The psalmist, according to the evidence of the psalm, is in a serious plight. His condition and position are such that there is a possibility that he may be forsaken by his parents. But in the midst of such a possibility he is not losing

81

heart entirely, for " when my father and my mother forsake me, then the Lord will take me up." Then he is opposed by enemies who, in order to make his discomfiture more complete, produce witnesses who perjure themselves. In the midst of such circumstances the psalmist has found strength in God, and out of his own experience he proclaims this message to all, "Wait on the Lord and you will receive all the strength you need." How does it work? I have to admit that I cannot give a full explanation. Yet what the psalmist said can be endorsed from personal experience and part of the explanation may be given in this way:

First, there is always strength to be gained in association with others. Unity is strength. What we may be afraid to undertake alone, we may be prepared to try if assisted by another. How much more, then, is this true when our Associate is God? Do not let anyone think that God is too far away and unreal to enter into life's difficulties with us. He is real, He is nearer than our hands or feet, nearer than the breath we breathe, and how much strength is imparted by being associated with Him! There can be no defeat when one is on the side of God.

And secondly, in His presence our spiritual vision is enlarged and our whole spiritual life is quickened, so that we are able to view things from the divine standpoint. Too often our vision is restricted by what takes place around us, and life assumes for us something that is much harder than it actually is because we are unable to see everything. The man in the valley can see no further than the surrounding hills, but the man on the hilltop can view not only the valley but the wider horizons. So it is with the man who waits in the presence of God. He is lifted above his ordinary circumstances. He views things through the eyes of

God, and so as he waits, he is indeed strengthened. Isn't it the psalmist who also said that he was distressed at the way the wicked prospered until " I went into the sanctuary then saw I their end "? You see, in the sanctuary, his vision was purified, clarified and enlarged. In other words, when we wait upon God we begin to view life through God and not God through life.

And thirdly, while waiting in the Divine Presence, there is a communication of the Divine Life. There is nothing surer than this—that the man who abides in the secret place of the Most High is possessed of divine power. He is gifted with spiritual energy far beyond those who only hastily rush in and then depart. He possesses a new poise for life because he is not so easily disturbed by passing circumstances. He dwells in the midst of the things of which there can be no change. No other explanation can be given than simply this—that God imparts Himself to those who wait upon Him.

And so this is the message: "Wait on the Lord, be of good courage, and He shall strengthen thine heart." The heart is the very centre of the whole personality. Thus the complete personality is strengthened and equipped, and so such an individual who hears this message and acts upon it finds that there is strength to continue the battle of life, no matter what its difficulties and its problems may be, no matter how great may be the sense of frustration.

And such an individual, too, becomes the possessor of the necessary strength to witness, for that is what the psalmist is doing when he begins to preach in this last verse—he is witnessing to the fact that his God is able to supply all his need in accordance with the riches in glory.

Let us finish with this note. In another psalm we read these words: "Rest in the Lord and wait *patiently* for Him." It is so easy to grow tired in waiting and, growing tired, lose all the benefits. "Wait patiently," says the psalmist, and they who thus wait are strengthened in heart.

Wait, then, I say, on the Lord.

EIGHTEEN

I WILL GO IN THE STRENGTH OF THE LORD GOD

Psalm 71:16.

THIS is a thought for us as we enter upon a New Year. How are we entering it? Is it with a sense of insecurity and uncertainty? Is it with the knowledge that temptation in all its power will seek to overcome us? Is it recognizing that we are beset with foes behind and before? If that happens to be the case, I ask again, how are we entering this year? We may step out with a measure of confidence in our own strength and ability. We can grit our teeth and by our own energies seek to overcome any of the difficulties that may arise in our path. But I am sure that is not true wisdom. Our Lord Himself gave us an illustration of the futility of trusting only to one's own endeavours. There may be a measure of success according to human standards, but to one such self-made man God had to say, " Thou fool."

On the other hand, we may be relying on others with the thought in our mind that united we stand.

There we may discover, however, that our unity may not last and even, should it hold, that our combined strength and capabilities are insufficient to cope with all the demands that life makes.

So I suggest that we begin this year, continue it and end it with this as our motto, " I will go in the strength of the Lord God." And let me here make one word of explanation lest I be misunderstood. That does not exclude my own efforts as well as the help that may be derived from others. It is the combination of all these under the direction of the Divine Will that is meant when we say, " I will go in the strength of the Lord God."

I will go, first, facing the uncertainty of the future in the strength of the Lord God. For the future is at all times uncertain. Not one of us has any idea what the future holds for us. We may have a good background of success upon which to build, but we cannot guarantee that success will continue. Our strength may have lasted out in the past, but we cannot claim that that strength will never fail us. Even Samson's strength failed him. And so, with all the uncertainty of the future to be faced, let us revive hope and confidence for the days that lie ahead and afresh take up the purpose that we have set before ourselves, by determining that we shall go forward only in the strength of the Lord God.

In the second place, facing temptations, I will go in the strength of the Lord God. Many have begun the year with new resolutions, and yet, though the year is only a few hours old, some of those resolutions have already been broken. I suggest they are broken simply because the individuals have relied upon their own ability to overcome. The psalmist makes no mistake in that way. Aware of his own inadequacy to cope with temptation alone, He has something different to suggest, and so he says, " I will go in the strength of the Lord." If we trust in Him in this way we shall find that what Paul says in 1 Corinthians 10:13 is true, " There hath no temptation taken you but such as is common to man: but God is faithful who will not suffer you to be tempted above that ye are able: but will with the temptation also make a way of escape that ye may be able to bear it."

Thirdly, facing foes, I will go in the strength of the Lord God.

When God commanded Joshua to lead his people into the Promised Land, this promise was made to him: " There shall not any man be able to stand before thee all the days of thy life "; and a similar promise is made in the words of Isaiah: " Behold all they which were incensed against thee shall be ashamed and confounded: they shall be as nothing: and they that strive with thee shall perish " (Isa. 41:11).

Men may think that they can overcome the child of God, and for a time it often appears as if they were able, but the soul that is in the safe keeping of God and goes forth into life in His strength has an assurance of having the Almighty constantly with him. " No weapon formed can harm the child of God."

Then, " A man's foes shall be they of his own household." When I quote this Scripture I am not thinking primarily of our closest relatives, although the fact of hostility within the home cannot be excluded, but I am thinking of the foes that are within us. How true we realize this to be when we have any accurate knowledge of ourselves! Our deadliest enemies are not those who are without, but those within. Jesus Himself gave us a terrible catalogue of the evils that come from within a man. " For from within, out of the heart of men, proceed evil thoughts, adulteries, fornications, murders, thefts, covetousness, wickedness, deceit, lasciviousness, an evil eye, blasphemy, pride, foolishness. All these evil things come from within and defile the man." But there is victory promised over such foes as well. "Sin shall not have dominion over you," says Paul. That, we know, can never be accomplished in our own strength, but it can be accomplished if we go in the strength of the Lord.

Let there be no doubting in this matter that there is fullness in Christ to provide strength for all, and for every occasion. "To the weak there comes strength, to the unholy, purity: to the perplexed, guidance, to the doubting, courage." It may be, someone complains, "Oh, but I am so weak!" To that I reply that is just the condition that Christ desires to see you in, because His word is this: "My strength is made perfect in weakness."

Shall we then seek the strength which the psalmist knew to be adequate for every situation? In the work to which God has called me, I long to be able to make the Christian message so real and clear to every audience that I address, that the hearers would want to experience it at its best for themselves. To come anywhere near accomplishing this, I know my dependence must be on God. It can never be accomplished in the power of human energy alone, and so as I go forth into another year, I intend taking the advice of the psalmist who obviously was not a young man, but one who had a vast experience of life. I say, I intend to take his advice and go forward in the strength of the Lord God.

Could we not go together?

NINETEEN

A CHRISTMAS MESSAGE

This address was preached on Christmas Day at a combined training centre to a party of officers and men of the Army and Navy, including W.R.N.S. and A.T.S. personnel.

THIS is Christmas morning. You, I am sure, agree that it is fitting that we should have a combined service. For all Protestant denominations, even although they may have a number of superficial differences, agree in the fundamental truths of the Christian faith, and the thought of which we are reminded on a day like this is one of these.

We gather to do honour and to worship God, who, because of His love for mankind, sent His Son into the world in human form. The Son came willingly to fulfil the will of His Father. Not much fresh thought can be brought to our notice on a day like this, but for the short time at my disposal I should like to refresh your memory upon two points that ask for our attention on Christmas Day.

First, the fact of which Christmas speaks.

Theologically, we call it the Incarnation. That is, God became man. Not that somehow man became God. God sent His Son, who Himself was divine, to take the form of human flesh and thus became man in order that He might be able to introduce us to God. In the New Testament, this fact is stated in different ways.

John, in his Gospel, uses current philosophical terms when he says, "The word became flesh and dwelt among us." Paul uses the language of theology when he says, "God was in Christ reconciling the world unto Himself."

To my mind, this amazing fact demands a remarkable birth, and the Christian Church holds that Christ's birth was remarkable. It goes by the name of the Virgin Birth. Now, I am quite aware that for many who have not accepted the Christian faith, and, indeed, for many who have, it is not easy for them to accept this doctrine.

It may be that many of us would agree with you when you refuse to accept as historical fact a Jewish maiden's story concerning the birth of her first child; yet before just casting it aside, I would ask you to consider the whole in this light. Carefully watch the Child of whom the story is told, follow His life until He became a man take note of all that He was able to do and achieve, stand beneath His Cross, and gaze upon that awful death, and then watch His empty tomb with at least 500 witnesses to attest the fact of His Resurrection. If the evidence thus produced brings you to acknowledge Him as a historical person and His resurrection as a historical fact, then I am sure you will find little difficulty in accepting the scriptural claims regarding His birth. Yea, indeed, such a life would demand just such a birth.

And then, secondly, the message of which Christmas speaks.

The central message of Christmas is, "Unto you is born a Saviour." From outside the world Jesus came to bring help to a needy, nigh despairing world and set it upon its feet again. That is what the world required in His day, and there are few of us but would agree that that is what the world needs to-day.

The remarkable thing about the message that God gives to humanity, either as spoken message or one given in the person of His Son, is its universal and age-long application, and this message has its application to the circumstances of to-day.

We all admit as we speak with one another, that the world is faced with tremendous difficulties, nor does it seem as if these difficulties would miraculously disappear nor gradually become less. When we discuss the condition of the world we realize that there are many theories expounded, not only concerning its condition but concerning its cure. But usually for us, our discussion ceases with the recognition that the problem is still unsolved, and as one officer said to me the other day, " it is a tremendous problem. I don't think any of us knows the answer."

Now, I believe with all my heart that this central Christmas message is the answer: "Unto you is born a Saviour." Tell me this: How do you explain the refusal of men to turn to Christ? They will turn to almost any " ism " and yet not turn to Him. He makes claims—tremendous claims—and He substantiates these claims, yet men, rather than give Him an opportunity of fulfilling the promises that He makes in their own lives, will turn, some to Fascism, some to Socialism and Communism, rather than give Him the chance that He has waited long to get. Still He continues to throw out invitations to all, and still He has, unfortunately, to say of men to-day as He said of them in His own day, " Ye will not come unto Me that ye might have life."

This Christmas season reminds us that God has provided a Saviour for everyone, and therefore for the world, and whosoever will may come and know Him in this way, for as Christ said Himself, " Him that cometh to Me I will in no wise cast out."

Now, Jesus Christ does not save in crowds, though

it is possible for a crowd to come to the knowledge of salvation together, but He seeks to become the Saviour of the individual. At the heart of the world problem is the heart of the individual. And Christ, recognizing this, stands at the door of each heart patiently waiting admittance so that He can create a new heart and a right spirit.

Yet we may refuse Him entrance as many do and become unconcerned to His persistent entreaty to be allowed to do for us what we cannot possibly do for ourselves. Thus the world is not in any way improved because the heart of the individual has not been changed.

A boy was given by his father a jig-saw puzzle to play with, to keep him employed while the father continued to study. In an incredibly short time the boy returned to the astonishment of the father, who hoped he would be kept employed for a long time, with the puzzle completed. To the father's question, " How did you complete the puzzle so soon? " the son replied, " It was a jig-saw puzzle of the world, but I noticed there was a man on the back, and when I got the man all right, the world was all right."

That is true. The world cannot be right until individuals are right. No one but God in Christ can effect this change. Why not on this Christmas Day give Him the opportunity to do this for you? It will have world-wide ramifications.

TWENTY

ALL POWER IS GIVEN UNTO ME IN HEAVEN AND IN EARTH ... GO YE AND TEACH ... AND LO, I AM WITH YOU ALWAY"

Matthew 28:18-20.

THESE are possibly some of the last words that Jesus spoke to His disciples.

The words of our friends are always valuable, but when it comes to the end, and they seek to get their last message to us, every effort is made not to lose a syllable of their final words, for we stress the importance of their last utterances. And though all the words of Jesus are of real value, it is only natural that we should be specially interested in His farewell message.

When I read these words and think for a moment of all that they visualize of power and authority, I feel it is tragic in the extreme that so many Christian people live on the verge of spiritual poverty when infinite resources are at their disposal and Christ is urging them to utilize every power offered to them.

Let me emphasize three points found in our text.

First, Christ's claim: " All power is given unto Me in heaven and in earth." You agree, I am sure, that this is a tremendous claim for any person to make. Not only is it power in heaven and not only power on earth, but it is both brought together with nothing excluded, for He says, " *All* power is given unto Me in heaven *and* in earth."

Take note of the occasion on which this claim was

made. It was after the resurrection. He did not make this claim when He was dying upon the cross. Even the disciples would have found it difficult to believe had He uttered these words as one of the sayings from the cross, for His death meant death to all their hopes. How could they continue to have faith and to believe in Him as One who possessed in His person all power when wicked men were able to put Him out of existence? But the claim was not made then, but after the cross, after death, after the grave, after the resurrection which they had all seen and believed.

The victory achieved in the resurrection substantiated the claim that He was now making. Not only so, it was in keeping with some of the other remarks that they had not quite understood, as, for example, " I and the Father are one "; or, when He spoke about His life, "No man taketh it from me: I have power to lay it down and I have power to take it again " (John 10 : 18). Looking out into the world to-day, it may be that many thinking people are inclined to accuse Christ of not utilising His power, at least the power He claimed to possess, and in a measure one can sympathise with them in their outlook, yet the Christian, knowing his Lord, believes that everything somehow is in the hollow of His hand; He believes that "Jesus shall reign where'er the sun does his successive journeys run ": he believes that Christ is coming again to this earth to *reign*.

And secondly, Christ's command, " Go and teach." To every disciple of Christ's, without exception, this command is issued. Our duty is to propagate the message which He left behind. Yet there are few Christians who undertake the sacred task in obedience to this command. That, however, does not alter the fact that wherever a disciple of Jesus Christ is to be found, there is laid upon him the necessity of proclaiming the mes-

sage in accordance with the desire of Christ. There
is work for every Christian man and woman.

To avoid any misunderstanding regarding the merit
of this work, let us carefully note this. We do not
work to save our souls, but we work because we have
been saved.

Let there be no mistake about this—the human can
do nothing to merit salvation. It is all of grace, but
once salvation has become the possession of any
individual, there need be no unemployment in Christian
service. No place is excluded. It is expected that every
place shall hear the message. So we are commissioned
to go and teach.

What shall we teach? Not what man's wisdom might
suggest should be taught, but what God teaches; in
other words, " What I have commanded you." Just
as Jesus Himself depended upon the Father for His
message, so, too, does the Christian. He is sent to teach
what God commands.

Then thirdly, Christ's promise: " Lo, I am with
you alway." Never is the child of God sent on the
Christian warfare on his own charges. He is not only
endued with power from on high, but he has constantly
the Possessor of all power with him. When an ambassador is sent to another country to represent his
king he is sent with full authority, but he leaves behind
the one who bestows the authority upon him. Yet the
wonder of the Christian experience is this, that not
only is he sent as an ambassador for Christ, but, as he
obeys, the King Himself accompanies in person His
ambassador. And the Christian can undertake nothing
aright apart from Him.

Notice again that the One who says, " Lo, I am with
you," is the one who also says, " All power is given
unto Me." What, then, can stand against the individual

who in the line of the divine will obeys the command and knows the fulfilment of this wonderful promise?

A dear old Christian lady found herself in the midst of some trouble. Her minister called upon her, and as he spoke he turned to this passage of Scripture and read again, "Lo, I am with you alway," and, turning to the old soul, he said, "Isn't it a gracious promise?" to which she immediately replied, "Yes, but it is more, for, to me, it is a blessed reality."

The Christian life thus seen becomes a challenge—a challenge to undertake all that Christ commands. Have we taken it up? If so, let us attempt anything and everything that He commands, for our resources are always equal to our needs.

It is almost impossible to turn to this passage of Scripture without remembering that it was David Livingstone's special text. You may remember that on one dark occasion in his experience in the heart of Africa, faced with the problem of advancing into hostile territory or making a retreat, he opened again his Bible as he sat alone in his tent towards midnight and read again these words, " All power is given unto Me; go ye . . . and lo, I am with you alway." Closing the book, he wrote in his diary, " It is the word of a Gentleman of the most strict and sacred honour, so there's an end of it."

May its message have a similar effect upon us so that even though we be tempted to turn back or to disobey His command, we shall be so renewed by the graciousness and the wonder of His promise to us that we shall go forward wherever He leads.